Kingdom Acceleration

Get Ready to be Released!

Ms. Alisha Jackson, MSW

For information about bulk orders, author events, or speaking engagements, please contact:

Healing Within Transformation Center
1321 Upland Dr. PMB 1515
Houston, Texas 77043 USA
Website: HealingWithinTransformationCenter.com
Email: support@healingwithintransformationcenter.com

Ms. Alisha Jackson, MSW
P.O. Box 572041
Dallas, Texas 75357 USA

Published in the United States of America by A Better Life Publishing Company
First Edition — 2026
ISBN: 979-8-98927684-4 (eBook)
ISBN: 979-8-9892768-7-5 (paperback)
Cover Design by Alisha Jackson

Editor by Charlyn Samson

A Better Life Publishing Company is a faith-based author supportive services program offered through Healing Within Transformation Center that supports creative freedom and Kingdom-inspired expression. Our mission is to empower authors to produce works that inspire spiritual growth, healing, and transformation while uplifting communities and advancing God's Kingdom throughout the world.

CONTENTS

DISCLAIMER

Kingdom Acceleration: Get Ready to be Released! is a faith-based motivational and self-help book inspired by personal experience, biblical principles, and divine revelation. It reflects the author's journey of transformation, healing, and spiritual growth. Some details, names, and events have been adjusted or summarized for clarity and confidentiality. The purpose of this book is to empower, inspire, and educate readers in their walk with God and in their pursuit of purpose.

This book is designed to offer guidance, encouragement, and spiritual development rooted in biblical truth. It may include professional insight from the author's background in social work and life coaching; however, it is not intended to replace personal, medical, psychological, financial, legal, or pastoral advice. Readers are encouraged to seek counsel from qualified professionals in these areas when needed.

Although the author is a Master Leveled Social Worker and Certified Kingdom Trauma and Transformational Life Coach, reading this book does not create a professional client relationship. The teachings and exercises within are meant for spiritual enrichment and self-development, not for the diagnosis or treatment of any condition.

The material presented is for **educational and inspirational purposes only**. Every effort has been made to ensure the accuracy and biblical integrity of the information shared. Individual results may vary depending on personal effort, spiritual growth, and obedience to God's guidance.

The author and publisher do not guarantee financial or business outcomes resulting from the application of any principles discussed in this book. All business or financial decisions should be made prayerfully and, when appropriate, with the advice of a licensed professional.

By reading *Kingdom Acceleration*, you agree to take full responsibility for your personal, spiritual, and business growth. Always remember—your success is guided by God's wisdom, faithfulness, and your willingness to walk in obedience to His Word.

DEDICATION

This book is dedicated to every courageous soul who dares to dream big, to those who believe that faith and business can coexist in beautiful harmony, and to those who are willing to step out in faith, even when fear whispers doubts. To the entrepreneurs, the leaders, the dreamers – the ones who are not afraid to use their God-given talents to build a kingdom that impacts the world. May these pages serve as a beacon of hope, a compass guiding you towards your divinely appointed destiny. May it be a source of strength and inspiration as you navigate the challenges and embrace the triumphs of your journey. This is for the warriors of faith, those who stand firm in the face of adversity and never give up on their God-ordained purpose. For my family, friends and clients, I dedicate this labor of love, praying that it equips and empowers you to reach new heights in your spiritual and professional endeavors. May your lives be a testament to the power of faith in action.

PREFACE

For years, I've had the privilege of witnessing firsthand the transformative power of faith interwoven with practical business strategies. As a Christian life coach and motivational speaker with a business background, I've seen countless individuals unlock their God-given potential to activate and achieve extraordinary success, both spiritually and professionally. But I also know the struggles and doubts many face, the battles fought in the marketplace, the seemingly insurmountable obstacles that threaten to derail even the most ambitious dreams. This book, *Kingdom Acceleration*, is born out of a desire to bridge the gap between faith and action. It's designed to equip you with the spiritual insights and practical tools you need to not only navigate the complexities of the business world, but to thrive in it while aligning your life with God's purpose. Within these pages, you'll discover not just inspirational messages, but actionable steps, proven strategies, powerful prayers, and practical exercises to help you clarify your purpose, overcome challenges, and build a business that reflects your Christian values. This is a journey of faith and entrepreneurship, a practical guide for those seeking to live out their faith in every aspect of their lives. Let us embark on this empowering adventure together, as we discover how to accelerate your kingdom impact.

INTRODUCTION

Are you a Christian entrepreneur or business professional yearning for a deeper connection between your faith and your career? Do you feel a calling to use your talents to make a tangible difference in the world? Do you sometimes feel overwhelmed by the challenges of balancing your spiritual life with the demands of building a successful business? If so, then *Kingdom Acceleration* is your roadmap to a more fulfilling and prosperous life. This book isn't just about making money; it's about building a kingdom – a thriving business that reflects your values, serves your community, and honors God in all you do. We'll explore the power of aligning your business with God's purpose, discovering and utilizing your unique spiritual gifts, and navigating the inevitable spiritual battles that arise in the marketplace. You'll learn practical strategies for overcoming obstacles, silencing distractions, and cultivating kingdom confidence. We'll delve into the importance of self-care, setting boundaries, and renewing your mind through the Word of God. Throughout this journey, you will be equipped with powerful prayers, affirmations, and practical tools designed to help you overcome challenges, cultivate a positive mindset, and achieve your God-given potential. This is more than a book – it's a partnership, a supportive guide for your personal and professional transformation. Prepare to unlock a new level of success, both in your business and in your relationship with God. Let's begin this exciting journey together!

CHAPTER 1

Laying the Foundation: Aligning Your Business with God's Purpose

DISCOVERING YOUR GOD-GIVEN PURPOSE AND TALENTS

Before we embark on building a kingdom-focused business, a strong foundation is crucial. This foundation rests upon the bedrock of understanding your God-given purpose and the unique talents He has bestowed upon you. Many entrepreneurs, driven by ambition and a desire for success, often overlook this critical first step. They rush into business plans, marketing strategies, and networking events without taking the time for quiet reflection and discerning God's will for their lives and businesses. This is akin to building a house on shifting sand—no matter how grand the structure, it's ultimately unstable.

Let's shift our perspective. Imagine you are a master craftsman, meticulously crafting a magnificent piece of furniture. You wouldn't begin hammering nails without first selecting the finest wood, understanding its grain, and envisioning the final masterpiece. Similarly, before you launch your business, take the time to understand the unique "wood" God has given you—your spiritual gifts and talents—and how they can be shaped into a beautiful and enduring testament to His glory.

This journey of self-discovery begins with prayer and introspection. Set aside a dedicated time for quiet reflection, perhaps in a peaceful setting like a quiet corner of your home, a nature walk, or a spiritual retreat. Engage in earnest prayer, asking God to reveal your unique gifts and how He intends for you to use them to build His kingdom. He has a plan for you, a purpose uniquely tailored to your strengths and passions. He doesn't want you simply to make a living; He wants you to live a life of purpose, a life that glorifies Him and leaves a lasting impact on the world.

To guide this process of self-discovery, consider engaging in some practical exercises. Many excellent personality assessments can help you identify your strengths and weaknesses. Tools such as the Myers-Briggs Type Indicator (MBTI) or StrengthsFinder can help illuminate your natural inclinations and talents. Remember, these assessments are tools to aid your understanding; they aren't definitive pronouncements of your destiny. The key is to integrate these insights with prayerful reflection and discern how your strengths align with God's plan for your life.

Journaling is another powerful tool. As you engage in self-reflection, take time to write down your thoughts, feelings, and insights. Ask yourself questions like: What am I passionate about? What activities bring me joy and fulfillment? Where do I see myself making a real difference in the world? What problems can I solve using my skills and abilities? What are my unique talents and gifts? How can I use my professional skills to further God's kingdom? These questions, coupled with prayerful consideration, will illuminate the path forward.

Let's explore some biblical examples of individuals utilizing their God-given talents for His kingdom. Consider Joseph, who used his gift of interpretation to save his family and a nation from famine. His ability to interpret dreams, a seemingly "ordinary" talent, became an extraordinary instrument in God's hands, preserving countless lives. Or take David, a shepherd boy with a slingshot, whose courage and skill brought down a giant and ultimately became king. His seemingly humble beginnings concealed a remarkable ability to lead and inspire.

These biblical figures remind us that God often uses ordinary individuals with seemingly ordinary talents to accomplish extraordinary things. He doesn't require extraordinary circumstances; rather, He seeks faithful hearts willing to use their gifts for His glory. Your unique blend of talents, however seemingly insignificant they may appear, is essential to God's plan.

Don't underestimate the power of your skills. Perhaps you excel at organization, communication, or problem-solving. Maybe you possess a gift for creativity, innovation, or compassion. These skills are not just secular assets; they are spiritual gifts, tools entrusted to you by God for His purpose. Think about how these talents could be utilized in a business context. Could your organizational skills help streamline processes in a non-profit? Could your communication talent create effective marketing campaigns for a faith-based organization? Could your creativity develop innovative solutions for social challenges? The possibilities are vast, limited only by our imagination and our willingness to listen to God's guidance.

It's vital to understand that discovering your God-given purpose isn't a one-time event; it's an ongoing journey of self-discovery, guided by the Holy Spirit. As you grow in your faith and experience, you'll gain deeper insights into your gifts and how best to utilize them. Remain open to God's direction, and be willing to adjust your course as you learn and grow. He may lead you in unexpected directions, unveiling opportunities you never anticipated.

The process of identifying your spiritual gifts might involve some introspection and self-assessment, but it is a journey well worth undertaking. It is a crucial step in aligning your business with God's purpose and building a sustainable, faith-based enterprise that reflects His glory. Remember, your talents are not just for your personal success; they are tools to build His kingdom, to bless others, and leave a legacy that extends far beyond your own lifetime.

This journey of self-discovery is not a solitary one. Engage in conversations with trusted mentors, pastors, or spiritual advisors. Their guidance and insights can provide valuable perspective and help you navigate the complexities of discerning God's will. Furthermore, engage in prayerful reflection with your community of faith. Their prayers and support can provide strength and encouragement during this transformative process. Don't be afraid to ask for help, as God often works through the people in your life.

Moreover, remember the importance of continuous learning and growth. Throughout your life, God may reveal new talents, skills, and opportunities that align with His purpose for you. Stay receptive to these revelations and be willing to embrace new challenges and adjust your course accordingly. Growth is an ongoing process, and your path to fulfilling your God-given purpose will likely evolve over time.

In conclusion, discovering your God-given purpose and talents is paramount to establishing a thriving, kingdom-focused business. This process involves dedicated self-reflection, prayerful consideration, and practical exercises designed to illuminate your unique strengths. Through studying biblical examples of individuals who used their talents for God's glory, we are reminded that even seemingly ordinary abilities, when wielded in obedience to God, can produce extraordinary results. This journey is not about solely focusing on financial success but about creating a business that is a reflection of God's love, grace, and compassion towards others. Embrace this journey with faith, persistence, and a heart surrendered to God's will, and witness the remarkable transformation in your life and business.

BUILDING A KINGDOM-MINDED BUSINESS PLAN

Now that we've established a strong foundation by identifying your God-given purpose and talents, let's move on to crafting a business plan that reflects those values. This isn't just about maximizing profits; it's about building a kingdom-minded enterprise that blesses others and glorifies God. Think of this plan as a roadmap, guided by prayer and divinely inspired wisdom, leading you towards a business that aligns perfectly with your spiritual calling.

The first step is to define your mission statement. This isn't a generic statement; it's a concise declaration of your business's purpose, reflecting your faith and values. It should clearly articulate how your business will contribute to the Kingdom. For example, instead of simply stating, "To provide excellent customer service," a kingdom-minded mission statement might read, "To provide exceptional customer service built on compassion, integrity, and a commitment to serving others as Christ served us."

Next, conduct thorough market research. Understand your target audience, their needs, and how your product or service can uniquely address those needs. Prayerfully consider how your business can offer value that extends beyond mere financial transactions—how can you contribute to the well-being of your customers and the community? This research isn't just about numbers and statistics; it's about recognizing the people behind the data and seeing them as individuals created in God's image.

Developing your marketing strategy involves crafting a message that resonates with your target audience while remaining true to your faith-based values. Avoid employing manipulative tactics or exploiting vulnerabilities. Instead, focus on building trust and transparency in all your communications. Think about how you can authentically connect with your customers and demonstrate your commitment to ethical and responsible business practices. Consider the use of testimonials, highlighting how your business has positively impacted individuals and communities.

Financial projections are essential, but they should be balanced with a perspective that transcends mere profit. While financial success is important for sustainability, remember that your ultimate aim is to build God's Kingdom. Consider integrating elements of philanthropy into your business model, such as donating a portion of your profits to charitable causes or incorporating fair-trade practices. Incorporate prayer into your financial planning, seeking God's wisdom in making wise and responsible decisions.

The operational plan details the day-to-day running of your business. This includes outlining processes, procedures, and systems. Ensure that your operational plan reflects your values of integrity, fairness, and compassion. Consider implementing fair labor practices, offering competitive wages, and providing a supportive work environment that fosters employee growth and well-being. Remember to pray for your employees, seeking guidance in building strong, positive relationships that honor God.

Regarding legal and regulatory compliance, ensure your business operates within the confines of the law and ethical principles. This goes beyond simply meeting minimum requirements; it involves a commitment to upholding justice and fairness in all your dealings. Consult with legal professionals who can provide guidance on navigating various legal and regulatory frameworks while maintaining your faith-based principles.

A strong team is essential for building a thriving kingdom-focused business. Surround yourself with individuals who share your values and commitment to serving others. Prayerfully select team members who not only possess the necessary skills and experience but also demonstrate character and integrity. Consider creating a company culture that emphasizes collaboration, mutual respect, and a shared commitment to your mission.

Community engagement is a cornerstone of a kingdom-minded business. Identify ways your business can actively contribute to the well-being of the community. This could involve sponsoring local events, partnering with non-profit organizations, or simply volunteering your time and resources. This engagement isn't just about corporate social responsibility; it's about embodying Christ's love and compassion in your interactions with the community.

Risk management is crucial, but it shouldn't paralyze you with fear. Prayerfully identify potential risks and develop contingency plans. This involves proactively addressing challenges and developing strategies to mitigate potential negative outcomes. Trust in God's provision and guidance as you navigate uncertainties.

The exit strategy—while often overlooked—is a crucial component of a long-term business plan. Consider how you want your business to transition in the future. Do you envision selling it to another kingdom-minded entrepreneur? Do you plan to pass it on to family members? Or will it eventually transition into a non-profit organization? Prayerfully consider the long-term implications of your exit strategy, ensuring its alignment with your values and commitment to building God's Kingdom.

Throughout the entire process of creating your business plan, remember to continuously seek God's guidance. Regular prayer, Bible study, and fellowship with other believers will provide the spiritual foundation for your business decisions. Pray for wisdom, discernment, and the strength to navigate challenges. Incorporate spiritual disciplines like fasting and meditation to deepen your connection with God and receive His divine guidance.

Let's explore some real-world examples of businesses that successfully integrate faith-based principles into their operations. Consider companies that prioritize fair wages, ethical sourcing, and community involvement. Many businesses demonstrate a commitment to environmental sustainability, reflecting a stewardship of God's creation. Research organizations dedicated to ethical business practices and social responsibility. Analyzing their strategies can provide valuable insights and inspire your own approach. These examples demonstrate that a profitable business can also be a powerful instrument for good in the world.

Remember, building a kingdom-minded business isn't just about profits; it's about leaving a legacy that glorifies God and blesses others. It's about integrating faith into every aspect of your business, from your mission statement to your exit strategy. It's about creating a business that embodies the values of love, compassion, integrity, and service. It's about using your gifts and talents not just for personal gain but for the advancement of God's Kingdom.

Finally, building a kingdom-minded business is an ongoing process, not a destination. As your business grows and evolves, continue to seek God's guidance and adjust your strategies accordingly. Remain flexible, adaptable, and open to His leading. Embrace challenges as opportunities for growth and learning, trusting in God's provision and guidance throughout the journey.

This detailed approach to business planning, grounded in faith and practical strategies, will empower you to build a thriving enterprise that not only succeeds financially but also reflects God's values and purpose. Remember, your business is not just a means of generating income; it's a platform for sharing God's love and making a positive impact on the world. Embrace this journey with faith and courage, and watch as God blesses your efforts beyond your expectations. Remember to always pray for guidance and wisdom, for discernment and understanding, and for His continued blessings upon your endeavors. The road may have challenges, but with faith in God, your journey of building His Kingdom will be a richly rewarding and fulfilling experience.

OVERCOMING FEAR AND DOUBT THROUGH FAITH

Fear. Doubt. These twin shadows often loom large over entrepreneurs, threatening to stifle the very spark of innovation and ambition that ignited their business dreams. But what if I told you that the antidote to these crippling emotions isn't found in elaborate business strategies or market analyses alone, but in the unshakeable foundation of faith? This isn't about blind optimism; it's about tapping into a power far greater than ourselves, a power that can transform fear into faith and doubt into unwavering trust.

The entrepreneurial journey is inherently risky. Failure is a real possibility, and the financial stakes can be high. It's easy to get caught up in the "what ifs"—what if I fail? What if I lose everything? What if my competitors outmaneuver me? These anxieties are perfectly normal; they're part of the human experience. However, allowing these fears to paralyze you is a choice, a choice that can be overcome through faith.

The Bible speaks extensively about overcoming fear. Proverbs 3:5-6 (KJV) assures us, "Trust in the Lord with all thine heart; and lean not unto thine own understanding. In all thy ways acknowledge him, and He shall direct thy paths." This isn't a passive resignation; it's an active surrender. It's about recognizing our limitations and humbly acknowledging God's sovereignty in our lives and businesses. When fear creeps in, whispering its insidious doubts, we can choose to replace those whispers with the confident affirmation of God's promises.

Consider the story of David and Goliath. David, a seemingly insignificant shepherd boy, faced the daunting task of battling a giant warrior. His faith, his unwavering trust in God's power, was the weapon that allowed him to overcome seemingly insurmountable odds. He didn't rely on his own strength or skill; he relied on God's strength and guidance. This reminds us that our faith isn't about our own capabilities; it's about tapping into a divine resource that surpasses all human limitations.

Financial insecurity is another major source of anxiety for entrepreneurs. The uncertainty of income, the pressure to meet financial obligations—these stressors can be overwhelming. But faith offers a perspective shift. It reminds us that God is our provider, the source of all blessings. Philippians 4:19 (KJV) reminds us, "But my God shall supply all your needs according to His riches in glory by Christ Jesus." This isn't a promise of instant wealth, but a promise of provision—sufficient resources to meet our needs, whatever they may be.

This faith-based perspective doesn't preclude diligent financial planning and smart business decisions; in fact, it enhances them. Prayerful consideration of financial strategies, seeking God's wisdom in investments and resource allocation, becomes a crucial part of the process. This is not about ignoring financial realities; it's about approaching them with a heart of faith, believing that God will guide our steps and provide for our needs.

Competition is another area where fear and doubt can take root. Seeing successful competitors can trigger feelings of inadequacy and self-doubt. But faith teaches us that we are not competing against others, but working towards a common goal—building God's kingdom. Our focus should be on excellence in our own sphere of influence, offering the best possible products or services and building authentic relationships with clients.

In a competitive marketplace, faith allows us to approach our work with an attitude of service, rather than competition. We are called to be stewards of our businesses, using our gifts and talents to bless others and to further the mission that God has placed on our hearts. Instead of being consumed by the anxieties of competition, we can choose to focus on what we are able to control—our own efforts, our own integrity, and our own commitment to excellence. This doesn't mean ignoring the market or competitors but rather viewing them with a changed perspective – recognizing the hand of God at work in all things.

Managing stress and building confidence are crucial aspects of the entrepreneurial journey. Spiritual practices like prayer, meditation, and Bible study can be powerful tools in cultivating inner peace and resilience. Regular prayer allows us to connect with God, to pour out our anxieties, and to receive His comfort and guidance. Meditation helps us to quiet our minds and focus on the present moment, reducing stress and anxiety. Bible study provides us with spiritual nourishment and wisdom, helping us to build a strong spiritual foundation to weather life's storms.

Beyond these practices, actively nurturing our faith through community involvement, fellowship, and service plays a crucial role. Connecting with like-minded believers provides support, encouragement, and accountability, transforming isolation into strength. Through service to others, we shift our focus away from our own anxieties and onto the needs of those around us. This service could involve volunteering within your community or providing opportunities for your employees to participate in meaningful service projects.

Spiritual warfare plays an equally important role in countering negative thoughts and emotions. Recognizing that spiritual forces can influence our thought patterns and actions allows us to actively employ the weapons of spiritual warfare: prayer, faith, and the Word of God. We actively resist the thoughts of doubt and fear, replacing them with God's truths, His promises, and His encouragement.

Journaling offers a powerful method for personal reflection and self-discovery. Regularly writing down our thoughts, feelings, and prayers allows us to process our emotions, identify areas where faith is lacking, and track our spiritual growth. By committing to consistent reflection through journaling, we can identify the root of our doubts and fears, addressing them with prayer, scripture, and faith-building practices. This allows us to engage in a personal process of spiritual transformation, moving beyond the anxieties that hinder us and instead stepping forward with renewed strength and confidence.

Moreover, remember to incorporate self-care into your daily routine. This means prioritizing physical and emotional well-being. Getting enough sleep, eating nutritious food, and exercising regularly helps to improve our overall health and resilience. Setting boundaries to protect your time and energy is essential to avoid burnout and maintain a healthy work-life balance. These aren't luxuries, but vital components of a thriving life, both spiritually and professionally.

In conclusion, overcoming fear and doubt through faith isn't a passive acceptance of fate. It's an active process of aligning our hearts and minds with God's will, trusting in His promises, and employing spiritual disciplines to build our resilience. It's about harnessing the power of faith to transform fear into courage, doubt into confidence, and anxiety into trust. As we embrace this journey of faith, we can not only navigate the challenges of entrepreneurship but also experience a deeper connection with God, a more profound sense of purpose, and a more rewarding and fulfilling life. The journey may be challenging, but with faith as our guiding light, the destination is a life of purpose, prosperity, and profound spiritual growth.

THE POWER OF PRAYER AND AFFIRMATIONS FOR KINGDOM BUSINESS

Prayer and affirmations are not mere spiritual exercises; they are powerful tools that can reshape our perspectives, bolster our confidence, and unlock unprecedented levels of success in the business world. They are the secret weapons of the faith-filled entrepreneur, providing a lifeline to divine guidance and empowerment in the midst of challenges. This isn't about replacing hard work and strategic planning; it's about augmenting them with a spiritual foundation that provides unwavering strength and resilience.

Let's start with prayer. Prayer isn't just a last resort when things go wrong; it's a constant conversation with God, a partnership where we seek His wisdom, guidance, and provision in every aspect of our business. Consider it less as a pleading and more as a collaborative dialogue, a seeking of His will and a yielding to His plans.

Think about the daily decisions you face as a business owner: Should you pursue a new venture? How should you handle a difficult client or employee? What pricing strategy is most appropriate? These aren't trivial matters; they can significantly impact the trajectory of your business. Prayer provides a pathway to discernment, allowing you to tap into a wisdom that transcends human limitations. It's about seeking God's will for your business, aligning your decisions with His purpose, and trusting in His guidance to lead you toward the best possible outcomes.

Here are examples of prayers you can adapt and personalize for your own business needs:

> **Prayer for Guidance:** "Heavenly Father, I come before You seeking Your wisdom and guidance in [specific business decision]. I ask that You illuminate my path, revealing the choices that align with Your perfect will for my business and Your kingdom. Give me discernment to make sound judgments, and grant me the courage to follow Your leading. In Jesus' name, Amen."

Prayer for Protection: "Lord, I thank You for the protection You provide over my business. I pray for Your divine shield against any harm, negativity, or setbacks that may threaten its success. Protect my employees, my clients, and my resources. Keep me from harm and guide me away from any dangerous or harmful ventures. In Jesus' name, Amen."

Prayer for Provision: "Father God, I acknowledge You as the source of all blessings. I pray for Your abundant provision for my business. Provide me with the resources I need, the clients I need and the opportunity to expand my business in line with Your plan. Bless my work, and use my business to further Your kingdom. In Jesus' name, Amen."

Prayer for Overcoming Obstacles: "Lord, I face [specific business challenge]. I ask for Your strength and guidance to overcome this obstacle. Grant me the wisdom to find creative solutions, the courage to persevere, and the faith to trust in Your perfect timing. Help me to see this challenge as an opportunity for growth and greater reliance on You. In Jesus' name, Amen."

These are just starting points; feel free to personalize them to reflect your specific circumstances and needs. The key is consistency—making prayer a regular part of your daily routine, not just a reactive response to crises. This constant communion fosters a deep relationship with God, providing continual guidance and support.

Equally crucial is the power of positive affirmations. Affirmations are powerful statements that reinforce positive beliefs and counter negative thought patterns. They reprogram your subconscious mind, helping you cultivate a mindset of faith, confidence, and success. Affirmations aren't about ignoring challenges; they are about facing them with a resolute spirit, fueled by unshakeable faith in God's ability to work through any situation.

Here are some examples of affirmations you can use daily:

"I am a successful entrepreneur, blessed and guided by God."

"My business is thriving, bringing glory to God and blessing to others."

"I am confident in my abilities, empowered by the Holy Spirit."

"I am attracting abundant clients and opportunities aligned with God's purpose."

"I am overcoming every obstacle with faith, resilience and God's strength."

"I am filled with peace, joy, and gratitude for God's blessings."

"God's wisdom guides my decisions, and His provision meets all my needs."

"I am a vessel of God's purpose, using my business to make a positive impact on the world."

"God's favor is upon my business, and I am experiencing continuous growth and success."

"I am surrounded by God's love, protection, and support in all that I do."

Repeat these affirmations multiple times daily – in the morning, during your workday, or before bedtime. You can write them down, say them aloud, or even record yourself saying them and listen to the recording. The consistency of repeating these affirmations daily is crucial to effectively reprogram your thinking patterns.

The combined power of prayer and affirmations creates a potent synergy. Prayer connects you to the divine source of strength and guidance, while affirmations reprogram your mind to embrace a mindset of faith and success. The result is a powerful combination that enhances your resilience, sharpens your intuition, and unlocks your potential for remarkable business achievements.

Remember, the principle of financial stewardship is outlined in God's Word. You are to have spiritual discipline that cultivates a deeper relationship with God, empowering you to navigate the challenges and seize the opportunities that come your way. It's about aligning your business with God's purpose, allowing Him to use your endeavors to further His kingdom and to bless others in the process. This journey requires faith, persistence, and a willingness to embrace God's guidance. But the rewards—both professional and spiritual—are immeasurable. Through consistent prayer and affirmations, you'll discover a newfound confidence, resilience, and an unshakeable belief in your ability to achieve your goals, all while building a business that reflects God's values and honors His purpose. This integration of faith and business is not just a strategy for success; it's a path to a life of purpose, fulfillment, and lasting impact. Embrace the power of prayer and affirmations, and witness the transformative impact they have on your business and your life.

The journey of faith and entrepreneurship is a synergistic dance, and the steps we take in prayer and affirmation are crucial to mastering this intricate partnership. Let faith be your compass, prayer your guide, and affirmations your fuel, and watch as your business flourishes in God's abundant grace. Remember to incorporate these practices into your daily rhythm, allowing them to become an integral part of your business strategy and your life's journey. The consistent engagement with prayer and affirmation will not only boost your business but also cultivate a deeper spiritual foundation, leading to a more fulfilling and meaningful life. This integrated approach to business and faith is not simply about achieving success; it is about living a life that honors God and blesses others. It is a path of purpose, empowerment, and enduring spiritual growth. The more you integrate these principles into your life, the more profound the results will become. Keep practicing, keep praying, and keep affirming, and watch God's blessings unfold in your business and your life.

SPIRITUAL DISCIPLINES FOR BUSINESS SUCCESS

Building a thriving business requires more than just a sharp mind and a solid business plan. It demands resilience, clarity, and a deep well of inner strength to navigate the inevitable challenges and setbacks. While strategic planning and market analysis are crucial, a truly successful and fulfilling business journey requires a strong spiritual foundation. This is where spiritual disciplines come into play, acting as the bedrock upon which we build our entrepreneurial endeavors, infusing our work with purpose and empowering us to overcome obstacles with grace and unwavering faith.

Prayer, as we've already explored, is the cornerstone of this foundation. But it's not just about asking God for blessings; it's about cultivating a constant conversation, a partnership where we seek His wisdom, guidance, and strength in every aspect of our business. Imagine prayer as your daily business meeting with the ultimate CEO, the source of all wisdom and provision. This consistent communion builds trust, resilience, and an unwavering faith that empowers you to make informed decisions even in the face of uncertainty.

Beyond daily prayer, incorporating regular Bible study into your routine is essential. The Bible isn't just a historical document; it's a living, active word filled with wisdom, guidance, and inspiration. It provides a framework for understanding God's character, His principles for success, and His promises for provision. By studying scripture, we gain a deeper understanding of our purpose, our gifts, and how to align our business practices with God's values.

Find a quiet space, free from distractions, perhaps early in the morning before the demands of the day engulf you. Read a passage slowly, meditating on its meaning and allowing the words to sink deep into your heart. Journal your thoughts and reflections, exploring how the principles you've read apply to your business life. Consider using a study Bible that provides commentary and insights, or join a Bible study group to share your understanding with others and gain different perspectives. Remember, the goal is not merely to complete a certain number of chapters; it is to cultivate a relationship with God through His Word.

Consider incorporating spiritual practices like fasting. While often associated with religious observance, fasting, whether it be from food, specific media, or even particular activities, can be a powerful tool for spiritual clarity and focus. It creates space for introspection, allowing you to quiet the noise of the world and listen to the still, small voice of God. Fasting isn't about self-punishment; it's about prioritizing spiritual connection and seeking God's guidance in a deeper way. It allows you to break free from distractions and focus on the things that truly matter. During a fast, your heightened spiritual awareness can provide unexpected clarity and insights into business challenges, leading to creative solutions and strategic breakthroughs. Consider a partial fast, focusing on reducing consumption of certain things, rather than a complete fast, to help maintain productivity while increasing your spiritual focus. Always consult with your doctor before starting a fast, particularly a complete fast, especially if you have any underlying health conditions.

Integrating these disciplines into your already busy schedule might seem daunting. But the key is not to strive for perfection, but to make consistent progress. Start small. Perhaps commit to 15 minutes of prayer and Bible study each morning. Then gradually increase the time as you feel comfortable. Experiment with different times of day to see when you're most receptive to spiritual practices. Some find early mornings ideal, while others prefer evenings for quiet reflection. Remember that consistency is key. Even short, focused sessions are more effective than infrequent longer ones. The goal is to cultivate a consistent rhythm of spiritual disciplines into the fabric of your daily life.

Consider structuring your week. For example, Mondays could be dedicated to strategic planning and prayer for guidance. Tuesdays could involve focusing on client relationships and praying for protection and provision for them. Wednesdays could be dedicated to Bible study, reflecting on relevant passages for business challenges and opportunities. Thursdays might focus on team building and praying for your employees' success and well-being. Fridays might be a day for reflecting on the week's successes and challenges, giving thanks and preparing for the next week.

Creating a dedicated space for your spiritual practices is vital. This doesn't need to be a grand room; a quiet corner in your office or home, perhaps with a comfortable chair and your Bible, journal, and prayer list, will suffice. Ensure this space is free from clutter and distractions, allowing you to fully immerse yourself in your spiritual practices. It's a sanctuary where you can connect with God, seek His guidance, and find strength for the week ahead. This space should be peaceful and inviting, a place where you feel at ease and can fully focus your attention on spiritual matters.

Remember, spiritual disciplines aren't just about personal growth; they impact every aspect of your business. When you prioritize your relationship with God, you're not just improving your spiritual life; you're enhancing your leadership, improving your decision-making, increasing your resilience, and building a stronger, more purpose-driven business.

Think of it this way: your business is a ministry. Whether you're selling products, providing services, or leading a team, you're impacting lives. By grounding your business in faith, you're not just striving for profit; you're building a kingdom enterprise. Your success is then measured not only by financial metrics but by the positive impact you have on others, the lives you've touched, and the glory you bring to God.

Integrating spiritual disciplines is a journey, not a destination. There will be days when you feel overwhelmed, distracted, or discouraged. But the key is to persevere, to keep returning to your spiritual practices, and to trust in God's unwavering guidance. The rewards of a life and business lived in alignment with God's purpose are immeasurable, offering not only professional success but also deep personal fulfillment and a sense of lasting impact. Remember, it's a marathon, not a sprint. Consistent dedication to these spiritual practices will yield abundant rewards in both your business and your personal life. Keep practicing, keep praying, and keep trusting in God's plan for your life and your business.

CHAPTER 2

Spiritual Warfare in the Marketplace

IDENTIFYING AND COMBATING SPIRITUAL OPPOSITION

Building a kingdom-focused business, as we've discussed, requires more than just shrewd planning and diligent execution. It demands spiritual acuity, a keen awareness of the unseen forces that can either propel or impede our progress. This isn't about succumbing to superstition; rather, it's about acknowledging the reality of spiritual warfare, a battle waged not just in the boardroom but also in the realm of the spirit. The marketplace, with its cutthroat competition and relentless pressure, can become a fertile ground for spiritual attacks aimed at derailing our God-given purpose.

Understanding spiritual warfare isn't about fear; it's about empowerment. It's about equipping ourselves with the spiritual armor described in Ephesians 6:10-18, a metaphorical suit of protection against the schemes of the enemy. This armor isn't physical; it's spiritual, comprised of truth, righteousness, peace, faith, salvation, the Word of God, and prayer.

Let's consider a scenario: Imagine you've poured your heart and soul into launching a new product, a project born from prayer and meticulous planning. Initial sales are promising, but suddenly, without explanation, orders plummet. Negative online reviews appear, seemingly out of nowhere. Key team members experience unexpected burnout or even resignations. Your enthusiasm begins to wane, replaced by a gnawing sense of discouragement and self-doubt. This, my friends, is a classic example of potential spiritual opposition at play. It's not simply bad luck or unfortunate timing; it's a deliberate attack aimed at thwarting God's plan for your business.

The Bible is replete with examples of spiritual warfare, from David's victory over Goliath to Paul's numerous encounters with adversity. These stories aren't just historical anecdotes; they are blueprints for navigating our own spiritual battles. They demonstrate that spiritual opposition is real, but so is God's power to overcome it. David's victory wasn't solely due to his physical prowess; it stemmed from his unwavering faith in God's promise and his reliance on divine strength. Similarly, Paul, despite facing imprisonment and persecution, persevered, fueled by his faith and the knowledge of God's unwavering support.

Recognizing spiritual attacks requires discernment, a spiritual sensitivity that comes from consistent prayer and Bible study. It's about learning to distinguish between natural challenges and supernatural opposition. Natural challenges, while difficult, are often the result of predictable factors like market fluctuations or unforeseen economic downturns. Spiritual attacks, however, feel different; they often involve sudden, inexplicable setbacks, a sense of overwhelming pressure, or internal conflict and discouragement that seems disproportionate to the external circumstances. They aim to discourage, to plant seeds of doubt, and to erode our faith.

One of the most effective weapons in our arsenal is the Word of God. The Bible isn't merely a collection of stories; it's a powerful tool for spiritual warfare. Memorizing scripture and declaring God's promises over our business is a vital defense against spiritual attacks. Think of it as deploying a shield of faith, deflecting the enemy's arrows of discouragement. Regularly reciting verses like Psalm 91, a powerful psalm of protection, or verses that affirm God's provision and guidance, will build a strong spiritual fortress around your business. Make it a daily practice, claiming these promises not only for yourself but for your team and your clients.

Prayer is another indispensable weapon. It isn't a passive activity; it's a dynamic engagement with God, a conversation where we seek His guidance, protection, and strength. Persistent prayer, whether during designated times of prayer or throughout your day, creates an atmosphere of spiritual warfare. We're not simply asking for things; we're engaging in spiritual combat, standing firm in faith against the enemy's assaults. Incorporate corporate prayer; pray with your team, uniting your faith and strengthening your collective resolve.

Furthermore, consider the power of fasting. As previously discussed, fasting, whether from food or other things, isn't about self-denial; it's about prioritizing spiritual connection and creating space for God to move powerfully in your situation. When facing an intense spiritual attack against your business, consider a focused fast, praying specifically for breakthrough and protection. This period of intentional spiritual focus can lead to unexpected clarity and insights, revealing blind spots and equipping you with creative solutions you may not have seen otherwise. Always remember to consult your doctor before undertaking any fast, especially if you have underlying health conditions.

Beyond prayer and the Word of God, cultivating a strong community of faith is crucial. Surrounding yourself with supportive believers who can offer prayer, encouragement, and accountability can significantly bolster your spiritual resilience. Share your challenges openly with trusted individuals; their prayers and wise counsel can provide vital support during times of spiritual warfare. Consider joining a business networking group with a strong faith-based component, where you can connect with fellow entrepreneurs who understand the unique challenges of building a kingdom enterprise.

Identifying the root of spiritual attacks is also crucial. Often, these attacks exploit weaknesses, vulnerabilities, or areas of unconfessed sin in our lives or in our business practices. Self-reflection, honest assessment, and repentance are vital steps in dismantling the enemy's foothold. Consider engaging in prayerful introspection, seeking God's guidance to identify any areas where compromise might be creating an opening for spiritual opposition. This is not about self-condemnation but about seeking divine healing and restoration.

Remember, spiritual warfare is not a solitary battle. God is our ultimate warrior, and He has equipped us with the necessary weapons to overcome. By embracing these spiritual disciplines—prayer, the Word of God, fasting, fellowship, and self-reflection—we can develop spiritual discernment, build resilience, and experience the power of God's intervention in the midst of challenging circumstances. As you navigate the complexities of the marketplace, remember that your faith is not a separate compartment of your life; it's the foundation upon which your business is built. And that foundation, grounded in Christ, is unshakeable. Your success is not just measured in profits and growth; it's measured in the lives you touch, the kingdom you build, and the glory you bring to God. Embrace the battle, claim victory, and witness the power of God in your kingdom enterprise.

Using Spiritual Weapons for Victory

Let's delve deeper into the practical application of these spiritual weapons, transforming abstract concepts into tangible strategies for navigating the complexities of the marketplace. We've established that spiritual warfare is real, and that it manifests in various ways—unexpected setbacks, sudden conflicts, and persistent feelings of discouragement, often disproportionate to the external circumstances. But how do we actively combat these attacks? How do we wield the weapons God has provided to secure victory?

Prayer, as we've discussed, is not merely a passive request; it's a dynamic engagement with the divine. Imagine you're facing a crucial business negotiation, a deal that could make or break your company. The stakes are high, the pressure is immense, and you sense an undercurrent of opposition, a feeling that something—or someone—is working against you. This is where targeted, strategic prayer becomes paramount. Instead of a general plea for success, engage in specific, focused prayer. Pray for clarity of thought, for wisdom in your communication, for God to soften the hearts of those you're negotiating with. Pray for His will to be done, knowing that even if the deal doesn't close, His plan is perfect.

Visualize the negotiation unfolding according to God's plan. Picture yourself speaking with confidence, presenting your ideas with clarity and grace, and finding common ground with the other party. This visualization, combined with persistent prayer, can create a powerful shield against the enemy's attempts to sow discord or confusion. Consider incorporating corporate prayer with your team before entering the negotiation. Unite your faith, and let the collective strength of your prayer become a tangible force in the room. This unified spiritual force can create an atmosphere that is conducive to agreement and a positive outcome. Remember, prayer isn't just about asking; it's about aligning your will with God's, trusting in His plan, and creating an environment where He can work powerfully on your behalf.

The Word of God is another indispensable weapon. It's not enough to simply read scripture; you must actively engage with it, memorizing key verses and declaring God's promises over your situation. In the context of our negotiation, consider verses that speak to peace, wisdom, and overcoming obstacles. Proverbs 16:3 (KJV), "Commit thy works unto the LORD, and they thoughts shall be established," becomes a powerful affirmation, reminding you that your plans are divinely ordained and will succeed if aligned with His will. Philippians 4:6-7 (KJV), "Do not be anxious about anything, but in every situation, by prayer and petition, with thanksgiving, present your requests to God" offers solace and strength in the midst of pressure. Regularly meditate on these verses, reciting them aloud before and during the negotiation, allowing their truth to permeate your heart and mind. This constant declaration of faith becomes a spiritual shield, deflecting the darts of doubt and fear.

Fasting, as a spiritual discipline, is not merely about abstaining from food; it's about prioritizing spiritual connection and creating space for God to work powerfully. When facing a particularly challenging business situation, consider a focused fast, praying specifically for breakthrough and wisdom. This period of intentional spiritual focus can lead to unexpected clarity and discernment. It's during these times of intentional spiritual focus that you may gain insights that you wouldn't have seen otherwise. During a fast, your spiritual senses become heightened, enabling you to perceive things that may have otherwise gone unnoticed. Remember to consult your doctor before undertaking any fast, particularly if you have underlying health conditions. This will be repeated throughout the book, to enforce you to take accountability of your health, get clearance medically, and have God assist you through it all. The goal of fasting is to enhance your spiritual awareness and connection with God, not to harm your physical health.

Consider a scenario where a competitor is aggressively undercutting your prices, threatening your market share. Instead of reacting with anger or fear, turn to prayer and fasting. Spend time in prayer, seeking God's wisdom and direction. Ask Him to reveal the root cause of this attack, whether it's a legitimate business strategy or a spiritual assault. During your fast, dedicate time to reading and meditating on scriptures that speak to God's provision and His ability to turn adversity into opportunity. This focused spiritual warfare can lead to creative solutions, such as developing a new marketing strategy or improving your product to better serve your target market. It might even reveal an unaddressed weakness within your own business practices that needs addressing.

The power of the Word, prayer, and fasting is amplified when combined with a strong community of faith. Share your challenges with trusted mentors, colleagues, or prayer partners. Their prayers and support can provide invaluable strength and encouragement during times of spiritual warfare. The collective power of faith can create a protective wall around your business, shielding it from spiritual attacks. Remember, you're not fighting alone; you have a vast spiritual army supporting you.

Finally, remember the importance of self-reflection. Spiritual attacks often exploit vulnerabilities in our lives, whether they are areas of unconfessed sin or unresolved emotional baggage. Honest self-assessment, coupled with repentance and reconciliation, is crucial in dismantling the enemy's foothold. Before any significant business decision, take time for self-reflection and prayer. Ask God to reveal any areas where your life is out of alignment with His will, and commit to making the necessary changes. This process of personal sanctification not only strengthens your spiritual resilience but also improves your overall decision-making process.

The marketplace can be a challenging arena, but armed with the spiritual weapons we've discussed—prayer, the Word of God, fasting, community, and self-reflection—we can not only overcome obstacles but also transform challenges into opportunities for growth and spiritual maturity. It's not about avoiding conflict, but about engaging in spiritual warfare with wisdom, discernment, and unwavering faith in God's power and provision. Remember, your business is not merely a means to an end; it's a ministry, a platform to serve others and build God's kingdom. Embrace this calling, and let your faith be the guiding force in all your endeavors. The victory is already won through Christ, and your role is to claim it through steadfast faith and courageous action. As you step into this arena, remember that you are more than capable. God has equipped you with everything you need to succeed, not just financially but spiritually, in fulfilling His purpose for your life and business. Embrace the power of the spiritual weapons He has provided, and watch Him transform your challenges into triumphs. Never forget that He is with you, always. And His plans for you are plans to prosper, not to harm; plans to give you hope and a future.

BUILDING A SHIELD OF FAITH AGAINST ADVERSITY

Let's now consider how to build an unshakeable faith—a shield against the relentless onslaught of adversity that often accompanies the entrepreneurial journey. The marketplace, while brimming with opportunity, can also be a crucible of intense pressure, unexpected setbacks, and seemingly insurmountable challenges. It's in these moments of crisis that the true strength of our faith is tested, and it's here that we must learn to rely not on our own resources, but on the unwavering power and unwavering promises of God.

Imagine this: You've poured your heart and soul into building your business, investing years of tireless work, countless sacrifices, and unwavering dedication. Suddenly, an unforeseen crisis hits—a market downturn, a critical component failure, a sudden lawsuit, a key employee departure. The weight of these challenges can feel crushing, threatening to dismantle everything you've worked so hard to achieve. Your emotions might range from fear and anxiety to anger and despair. In such moments, the temptation to succumb to doubt and discouragement can be overwhelming. But this is precisely where the power of faith becomes paramount.

Building a shield of faith is not about avoiding challenges; it's about confronting them with a heart fortified by God's strength and promises. It's about cultivating an unwavering belief in His sovereignty, His provision, and His unwavering love, even amidst the storm. This requires a proactive, intentional approach, not a passive hope that things will eventually work out. It demands a daily commitment to nurturing our spiritual lives, strengthening our connection with God, and aligning our actions with His will.

One critical element in building this shield is consistent prayer. We've already discussed the importance of strategic prayer, but let's explore it further in the context of facing adversity. When faced with a major setback, the natural inclination is to focus on the problem—the lost contract, the financial shortfall, the negative publicity. However, shifting our focus to God, seeking His wisdom and guidance, is crucial. Instead of dwelling on the negative, pray for discernment, clarity, and strength to navigate the situation effectively.

Prayer during challenging times is not just about asking for a miracle; it's about deepening our relationship with God, strengthening our trust in His plan, and seeking His will for our lives. It involves acknowledging our dependence on Him, relinquishing control, and surrendering to His sovereign plan. This act of surrender is not a sign of weakness, but rather a demonstration of profound faith and trust in His ability to work all things for our good. Consider setting aside specific times each day for prayer, dedicated to seeking God's direction and strength during the crisis. This focused prayer can become a source of unwavering strength, providing the spiritual stamina needed to endure and overcome the challenges.

Alongside prayer, immersing ourselves in the Word of God is vital. Scripture provides not only comfort and encouragement but also practical wisdom for navigating adversity. When confronted with difficult circumstances, spend time reading passages that speak to faith, hope, perseverance, and God's unwavering love. Consider verses like Psalm 23, which offers comfort and reassurance, or Psalm 46, which speaks of God as our refuge and strength. Let these scriptures become a source of spiritual nourishment, strengthening your faith and reminding you of God's promises.

Don't just passively read the scriptures; actively meditate on them, allowing their truth to sink deep into your heart and mind. Memorize key verses and declare them aloud, speaking God's promises over your situation. This act of faith creates a powerful spiritual shield, deflecting the darts of doubt and fear that the enemy often uses to discourage and defeat us. The more we immerse ourselves in God's Word, the stronger our spiritual foundation becomes, the more resilient we become to the challenges we face. This intentional engagement with scripture acts as a constant reminder of God's unwavering love and power.

Fasting, another powerful spiritual discipline, can be a crucial tool in times of adversity. While the physical aspect of abstaining from food can be challenging, the spiritual benefits can be profound. Fasting creates space for increased spiritual focus, allowing us to connect with God on a deeper level. It's a time for introspection, repentance, and seeking God's guidance. During a fast, we are more receptive to His voice, and more likely to receive His wisdom and direction. Remember to approach fasting prayerfully and with wisdom, seeking guidance from your pastor or a spiritual mentor.

Consider incorporating elements of corporate prayer into your response to adversity. Sharing your challenges with trusted friends, family, or members of your church community can be immensely beneficial. Their prayers and support can provide a powerful boost to your faith and strength. This collective spiritual force can create a shield of protection around you and your business, providing the support and encouragement needed to overcome challenges. Sharing your burdens with others also helps to prevent isolation, a feeling that can often intensify feelings of discouragement and despair.

Remember, self-care is not selfish; it's essential. During times of stress and adversity, it's crucial to prioritize your physical, emotional, and mental well-being. Get adequate rest, eat nutritious foods, exercise regularly, and engage in activities that bring you joy and relaxation. Neglecting your physical and emotional health will only weaken your spiritual resilience, making you more vulnerable to the enemy's attacks. Self-care isn't a luxury; it's a necessity, a critical component of spiritual warfare.

Finally, remember to continually examine your own heart and life. Spiritual warfare often exploits vulnerabilities in our character or our lives, areas where we have not fully yielded to God's will. Areas of unconfessed sin, unforgiveness, or bitterness can create openings for the enemy to gain a foothold. Honest self-reflection, coupled with repentance and reconciliation, is essential in dismantling these strongholds. Take time for personal prayer and reflection, asking God to reveal any areas where you are out of alignment with His will, and commit to making the necessary changes. This process of personal sanctification not only strengthens your spiritual resilience but also clarifies your decision-making process, enabling you to make choices that are aligned with God's purpose for your life and business.

The path of an entrepreneur is not always easy. There will be times of intense pressure, unexpected setbacks, and overwhelming challenges. But it is in these moments that the strength of our faith is tested and refined. By cultivating a shield of faith through consistent prayer, immersion in God's Word, fasting, corporate prayer, and self-care, we can face adversity with courage, resilience, and unwavering faith in God's power and provision. Remember, He is with you, always, guiding you, protecting you, and empowering you to overcome every obstacle. Trust in Him, and He will lead you to victory. Your journey, though challenging, is a testament to God's grace and your resilience, a story of faith overcoming adversity. Embrace the challenges, learn from the setbacks, and trust in the unwavering love and power of God to guide you to the success He has planned for you.

OVERCOMING DISCOURAGEMENT AND MAINTAINING A POSITIVE OUTLOOK

The entrepreneurial journey, as we've discussed, is a spiritual battlefield. While we've focused on building a robust spiritual defense, the fight isn't solely about repelling attacks; it's also about maintaining an unwavering, positive outlook – a vibrant offense against the enemy's attempts to demoralize and defeat us. Discouragement, that insidious whisper of doubt and despair, is a potent weapon in the adversary's arsenal. It seeks to chip away at our faith, erode our determination, and ultimately, paralyze our progress. But we are not powerless against this subtle assault. We possess a formidable weapon: a positive outlook rooted in faith and fueled by God's unwavering promises.

Maintaining a positive outlook amidst challenges isn't about ignoring the difficulties; it's about reframing our perspective, focusing on God's faithfulness even amidst the storm. It's about choosing to see the challenges not as roadblocks, but as opportunities for growth, refinement, and a deeper understanding of God's purpose for our lives. Consider the story of Joseph in the Old Testament. Sold into slavery by his brothers, falsely accused, and unjustly imprisoned, Joseph could easily have succumbed to bitterness and despair. Yet, he maintained an unwavering faith, trusting in God's plan even when his circumstances seemed utterly hopeless. His unwavering faith, his positive outlook despite adversity, ultimately led him to a position of immense influence and power, where he was able to save his family and his people from famine.

Joseph's story is a powerful illustration of the transformative power of a positive outlook. It reminds us that even in the darkest of times, God is at work, orchestrating events to bring about His ultimate purposes. Our challenges, however painful, are often part of a larger plan designed to shape us, refine us, and prepare us for greater things. Maintaining a positive outlook during difficult times requires intentional effort. It's a choice, a decision to focus on the good, the possible, and the promises of God, rather than dwelling on the negative, the seemingly impossible, and the uncertainties of the future.

One practical strategy for maintaining a positive outlook is cultivating an attitude of gratitude. When faced with difficulties, it's easy to become overwhelmed by the negative aspects of our situation. However, taking the time to consciously identify and appreciate the blessings in our lives, no matter how small, can significantly shift our perspective. This involves consciously shifting our focus from what we lack to what we have—our health, our family, our faith, our opportunities, our existing resources, and even the lessons learned from past mistakes. Keeping a gratitude journal, where you write down things you are thankful for each day, can be a powerful tool in cultivating this mindset. This intentional practice of acknowledging God's blessings helps to reframe our thinking and foster a sense of peace and hope.

Another crucial element in maintaining a positive outlook is surrounding ourselves with positive influences. The people we associate with can have a profound impact on our attitude and outlook. Choose to spend time with individuals who uplift, encourage, and support you, those who share your faith and inspire you to persevere. Conversely, limit your exposure to negative or pessimistic individuals who may drain your energy and reinforce negative thoughts. Cultivating a supportive network of faith-based friends, mentors, and accountability partners can significantly strengthen your resilience and help you maintain a positive perspective even during challenging times.

Furthermore, we must be mindful of our self-talk. The internal dialogue we engage in plays a crucial role in shaping our outlook. Negative self-talk, filled with self-doubt, criticism, and fear, can quickly undermine our confidence and motivation. Replace such negative thoughts with positive affirmations that align with God's promises and your identity in Christ. Regularly declare statements such as "I am strong in the Lord," "I am capable," "I am blessed," "God is my provider," "I can do all things through Christ who strengthens me," and others that reinforce your faith and resilience. This conscious effort to replace negative self-talk with positive affirmations is crucial in maintaining a positive outlook during challenging times.

Furthermore, engage in activities that bring you joy and restore your spirit. During stressful times, it's essential to maintain a healthy balance between work and relaxation. This means setting aside time for hobbies, activities, or interests that bring you joy and restore your energy. These activities can serve as a valuable refuge from stress, helping you recharge and maintain a positive perspective. Remember, self-care is not a luxury, but a necessity, a vital component of spiritual warfare. Prioritizing self-care will strengthen your physical and emotional resilience, making you better equipped to face challenges with a positive outlook. Regular exercise, sufficient sleep, healthy eating, and engaging in activities that rejuvenate your spirit are all crucial components of this vital aspect of maintaining a positive outlook.

Visualize your success. This powerful technique, rooted in faith and positive thinking, is a potent tool for maintaining a positive outlook. Regularly spend time visualizing yourself achieving your goals. Imagine the feelings of accomplishment, the joy of success, and the impact your business will have on others. This practice helps to strengthen your belief in your ability to succeed and reinforces your commitment to your goals. Pairing visualization with prayer can amplify its effects, creating a powerful synergy of faith and positive thinking.

Embrace the power of forgiveness. Unforgiveness can be a significant source of negativity and discouragement. It festers within us, poisoning our hearts and clouding our outlook. Forgiving others, and ourselves, is essential for maintaining a positive outlook. Remember, forgiveness is not about condoning wrongdoing, but about releasing the bitterness and resentment that can hold us back. Forgiveness frees us to move forward, unburdened by the weight of past hurts and resentments, allowing us to maintain a positive and hopeful perspective. This freedom is crucial to maintaining a proactive, positive outlook on your business and life.

Finally, remember the promises of God. The Bible is full of promises of strength, provision, guidance, and peace. During challenging times, intentionally meditate on these promises, claiming them for your life and your business. Remember verses such as Psalm 23 (KJV): "The LORD is my shepherd; I shall not want. He maketh me to lie down in green pastures: he leadeth me beside the still waters. He restoreth my soul:" or Philippians 4:13 (KJV): "I can do all things through Christ which strengtheneth me." These promises are not merely words on a page; they are living, active truths that can sustain us through adversity and empower us to maintain a positive outlook. Recite them, pray them, believe them, and allow them to become the foundation of your hope and resilience. Continue to work on your faith journey through personal development, at which you can learn more through AlishaJacksonAcademy.com, HealingWithinTransformationCenter.com, and/or FaithConnectionCenter.org for domestic violence surviving women with children under the age of 5 years old.

The entrepreneurial journey is a marathon, not a sprint. There will be times of discouragement, times when doubt creeps in and threatens to undermine our faith. But by employing these strategies—cultivating gratitude, surrounding ourselves with positive influences, monitoring our self-talk, prioritizing self-care, visualizing success, embracing forgiveness, and remembering God's promises— we can overcome discouragement and maintain a positive, hopeful outlook, even when faced with seemingly insurmountable challenges. Remember, your faith is your strength, your positive outlook is your weapon, and God's promises are your shield. With faith as your foundation, you are equipped to overcome any obstacle, achieving spiritual and professional success. Your journey, though challenging, is a testament to God's grace and your resilience, a story of faith overcoming adversity. Embrace the challenges, learn from the setbacks, and trust in the unwavering love and power of God to guide you to the success He has planned for you.

THE ROLE OF FORGIVENESS AND RECONCILIATION IN BUSINESS

Building a kingdom-focused business isn't just about profits; it's about building relationships, and relationships, like any living thing, require nurturing and, sometimes, repair. The marketplace, despite its often cutthroat reputation, is still comprised of people – people with flaws, shortcomings, and the capacity for both great kindness and deep hurt. Inevitably, conflicts arise. Disagreements over contracts, misunderstandings about expectations, personality clashes – these are all common occurrences in the business world. How we handle these conflicts, how we navigate the turbulent waters of interpersonal friction, is crucial to our spiritual and professional success. This is where the power of forgiveness and reconciliation takes center stage.

Forgiveness, in the business context, isn't simply a nice-to-have; it's a necessity. Holding onto resentment, anger, and bitterness towards a business partner, an employee, a client, or even a competitor, is like carrying a heavy weight that hinders our ability to move forward. This weight consumes our energy, clouds our judgment, and ultimately, impacts our productivity and our overall well-being. Unforgiveness creates a toxic environment, poisoning not only our own hearts but also the atmosphere of our business. It breeds mistrust, stifles creativity, and can even lead to legal battles and financial ruin.

The Christian faith provides a powerful framework for understanding and practicing forgiveness. It's not about condoning wrongdoing; it's about releasing the bitterness and resentment that bind us to the past. It's about choosing to break free from the chains of negativity and embracing the freedom that comes from letting go. Jesus Christ himself exemplified the ultimate act of forgiveness, sacrificing his life for the sins of humanity. This act of immeasurable grace serves as the ultimate model for our own forgiveness practices, both personally and professionally.

Consider the story of a small business owner, Sarah, who faced a significant conflict with her major supplier. The supplier consistently failed to meet deadlines, delivering substandard materials that threatened the quality of Sarah's products and jeopardized her reputation. Initially, Sarah was consumed with anger and frustration. She contemplated legal action, considering it a necessary defense of her business and her livelihood. But as she prayed, she realized that pursuing legal action wouldn't necessarily solve the underlying issues and might even escalate the situation further.

She remembered a sermon on forgiveness and its transformative power. It wasn't easy, but Sarah decided to approach the situation differently. She decided to meet with the supplier, not to accuse or condemn, but to express her concerns openly and honestly, while simultaneously seeking understanding. She listened patiently to the supplier's explanations, uncovering hidden issues such as unexpected family emergencies and equipment malfunctions. Through this empathetic dialogue, Sarah was able to see the supplier not merely as an adversary but as a fellow human being struggling with their own challenges.

With compassion and grace, Sarah collaborated with the supplier to create a plan for improvement. They worked together to address the supply chain issues, improving communication and establishing clear expectations. The supplier, touched by Sarah's understanding and willingness to collaborate, redoubled their efforts, consistently meeting deadlines and delivering higher-quality materials. The relationship, once strained and fraught with conflict, transformed into a partnership built on trust and mutual respect. The business prospered, not because of legal battles but because of forgiveness, grace, and a genuine desire to work collaboratively.

Reconciliation, the act of restoring broken relationships, is the natural outcome of forgiveness. It's the process of rebuilding trust, restoring communication, and renewing commitment. It acknowledges the hurt caused by conflict while simultaneously emphasizing the importance of moving forward together. In the business world, reconciliation can involve mediating disputes, renegotiating contracts, or even finding creative solutions to satisfy all parties involved.

Additionally, reconciliation doesn't necessarily mean forgetting what happened. It doesn't mean minimizing the seriousness of the offense. Rather, it means choosing to move beyond the conflict, focusing on rebuilding a healthy and productive relationship. It's a conscious decision to let go of the past and embrace the opportunity for a better future. This requires humility, empathy, and a willingness to compromise. It often involves a willingness to admit fault, even if it means swallowing one's pride.

Forgiveness and reconciliation are essential not only for resolving conflicts but also for preventing them. When we cultivate a culture of forgiveness and understanding within our businesses, we create a more harmonious and productive work environment. Employees feel more valued, empowered, and engaged, leading to increased loyalty, motivation, and overall performance. Clients perceive our company as trustworthy and reliable, fostering stronger relationships and enhancing brand reputation. Our partners and suppliers view us as collaborative and cooperative, leading to stronger alliances and a stable supply chain.

Applying these principles requires practical strategies. Open communication is crucial. Creating a safe and supportive environment where employees feel comfortable expressing their concerns without fear of reprisal is paramount. Regular team-building activities, fostering trust and understanding among team members, can significantly reduce the incidence of conflict. Providing conflict resolution training to employees empowers them to handle disagreements constructively and prevent minor disagreements from escalating into major conflicts.

Developing clear and transparent communication channels ensures everyone is on the same page. Regular check-ins with team members, clarifying expectations and addressing potential problems promptly, prevents misunderstandings from escalating. A written code of conduct, outlining expectations for ethical behavior and conflict resolution, ensures that everyone understands the company's commitment to a positive work environment.

Mediation can be a powerful tool for resolving disputes. A neutral third party can facilitate communication, helping conflicting parties to understand each other's perspectives and find mutually agreeable solutions. Mediation can be particularly useful in resolving conflicts between business partners, employees, or clients. Legal action, while sometimes necessary, should be considered a last resort. A collaborative approach to resolving conflict is often more beneficial in the long run, preserving relationships and avoiding costly legal battles.

Building a kingdom-focused business requires more than just financial success; it involves creating a thriving community, a place where people feel valued, respected, and supported. Forgiveness and reconciliation are not merely abstract concepts; they are essential tools for building strong, lasting relationships that underpin a thriving business. By embracing these principles, we not only enhance our personal well-being but also cultivate a more productive, harmonious, and ultimately successful business. Remember, your actions, guided by faith and compassion, can transform conflicts into opportunities for growth and strengthen your kingdom-focused business. Embrace the power of forgiveness, practice reconciliation, and witness the transformative impact on your business and your life. The journey of entrepreneurship is a spiritual journey, and the principles of love, grace, and mercy are not optional extras; they are fundamental building blocks of success.

CHAPTER 3

Transforming Pain into Purpose

IDENTIFYING PAST TRAUMAS AND HEALING FROM PAST HURTS

The foundation of a thriving kingdom-focused business, as we've explored, is built on strong relationships. But these relationships, both personal and professional, can be profoundly impacted by the weight of our past. Unresolved hurts, traumas, and limiting beliefs can subtly, and sometimes overtly, sabotage our efforts, hindering our ability to reach our full potential, both spiritually and professionally. Before we can truly accelerate our kingdom purpose, we must confront and heal from these past wounds.

This isn't about dwelling on negativity; it's about acknowledging the past so we can move forward, empowered and unshackled. It's about recognizing how past experiences shape our present actions and beliefs, allowing us to consciously choose healthier patterns moving forward. Think of it as spring cleaning for your soul, clearing out the clutter to make space for God's abundant blessings.

Identifying these past hurts requires introspection and honest self-reflection. It's a journey of self-discovery, guided by prayer and the illumination of the Holy Spirit. Start by asking yourself some key questions. What unresolved issues from your past are still affecting your present? Are there relationships that haven't been fully healed? What limiting beliefs – those negative, self-defeating thoughts – are holding you back? Are you carrying guilt, shame, or resentment that's preventing you from moving forward? These questions are designed to spark reflection, not to overwhelm. Take your time; answer them with grace and understanding.

Journaling is a powerful tool in this process. Write down your thoughts and feelings without judgment. Don't worry about perfect grammar or eloquence; the goal is to simply pour out your heart to God and yourself. As you write, you may start to identify patterns and recurring themes in your experiences. You might discover deep-seated hurts you weren't even consciously aware of. This process of uncovering and acknowledging these hurts is the first crucial step towards healing.

Prayer is paramount in this process. Ask God for wisdom and discernment to understand the root causes of your pain. Ask for strength and courage to face the difficult emotions that may arise. Remember, God's love is unconditional and unwavering. He doesn't condemn us for our past mistakes; He desires to heal us and set us free. Let His love wash over you as you engage in this vulnerable process of self-reflection. Pray for healing, for strength, for wisdom and clarity.

Consider incorporating scripture into your prayer. Verses like Psalm 147:3 (KJV), "He healeth the broken in heart, and bindeth up their wounds," offer comfort and assurance. Meditate on verses that speak to forgiveness, healing, and restoration. Allow these words of truth to penetrate your heart and renew your mind. These scriptures are not merely words on a page; they are promises from God, promises designed to bring comfort and hope in your journey of healing.

Sometimes, the wounds we carry are too deep to process alone. Seeking professional help from a Christian counselor or therapist is a sign of strength, not weakness. A trained professional can provide a safe and supportive environment where you can explore your past hurts in detail, developing healthy coping mechanisms and strategies for moving forward. They can help you identify and challenge limiting beliefs, replacing negative thought patterns with positive, faith-filled affirmations. They are equipped to guide you through this healing process with the knowledge and skills that assist in emotional, spiritual, and relational growth. Do not hesitate to seek this assistance; it's a demonstration of your commitment to your overall well-being.

Remember Sarah, from our previous example? While her story highlighted forgiveness within the business context, her success also depended on her own internal healing. Perhaps Sarah harbored underlying insecurities about her business acumen, rooted in past failures or criticisms. These insecurities, if left unaddressed, might have hindered her ability to respond with compassion and grace to her supplier's shortcomings. By acknowledging and addressing these deeper issues through prayer, journaling, or perhaps even counseling, Sarah would have further solidified her ability to navigate the challenges of entrepreneurship with resilience and faith.

Healing from past hurts is not a quick fix; it's a process. It requires patience, perseverance, and unwavering faith in God's restorative power. There will be days when you feel overwhelmed, when the pain resurfaces. But even in those moments, remember that you are not alone. God is with you, walking beside you every step of the way. He is your healer, your comforter, and your strength. Lean on Him, trust in His plan, and allow Him to guide you towards wholeness and freedom.

Let's delve deeper into some practical applications. Imagine you're dealing with the lingering effects of a past betrayal. Perhaps a business partner acted unethically, causing you significant financial and emotional harm. This experience may have instilled a deep distrust in others, making it difficult to form new partnerships or delegate responsibilities within your business. Through prayer and journaling, you might uncover the root of this distrust, acknowledging the pain and anger, but also recognizing the possibility of forgiveness and renewed trust. The journey might involve letting go of the need for revenge and choosing instead to focus on building healthier relationships, guided by faith and sound business practices.

Another example might involve overcoming the fear of failure, a common obstacle for entrepreneurs. This fear could stem from past experiences of rejection, criticism, or financial setbacks. Journaling can help unearth the source of this fear, allowing you to examine its validity. You can then begin to challenge those negative thoughts, replacing them with affirmations based on God's promises of strength, provision, and success. Through prayer and meditation, you can begin to cultivate a kingdom-focused mindset, trusting in God's guidance and allowing His love to overcome your fear.

The process might involve identifying specific limiting beliefs, such as "I'm not good enough" or "I'll always fail." These beliefs, often rooted in past experiences, can severely hinder your success. A Christian counselor can help you identify these limiting beliefs and develop strategies for challenging and overcoming them. Through faith-based cognitive behavioral therapy, you can reprogram your thinking patterns, replacing negative self-talk with positive, faith-filled affirmations that align with God's truth.

Healing is not about erasing the past but about transforming it. It's about integrating your past experiences into your present life, learning from them, and allowing them to shape you into a stronger, more resilient, and more compassionate individual. This journey will equip you not only to navigate the challenges of entrepreneurship but also to extend grace and understanding to others who are struggling. As you heal, you'll be better equipped to build genuine, lasting relationships that will underpin your kingdom-focused business. Remember, your past doesn't define your future; your faith does. Embrace the journey of healing, trusting in God's unwavering love and guidance, and watch as He transforms your pain into purpose. The transformation you undergo will empower you, not only personally, but also as a leader in your kingdom-focused business. The process is ongoing, a testament to your commitment to walking with God, aligning your life and business with His divine plan. Your healing journey is a continuous act of faith, where God's transformative power unfolds in your life, impacting not only your personal well-being, but the success and positive impact of your kingdom-focused business.

Using Your Testimony to Inspire Others

Your journey of healing isn't just a personal one; it's a powerful testimony waiting to be shared. The experiences that once held you captive, the hurts that once defined you, can now become beacons of hope for others. Sharing your story, your transformation from pain to purpose, is a profound act of faith, a testament to God's restorative power, and a catalyst for inspiring profound change in the lives of others.

Imagine standing before an audience, not as a victim of circumstance, but as a conqueror of adversity, a testament to God's unwavering grace. This isn't about seeking pity or attention; it's about offering hope, encouragement, and a tangible example of God's transformative power in action. Sharing your testimony is a powerful act of service, a way to extend the love and grace you've received to those who need it most.

This is particularly relevant in the context of building a kingdom-focused business. Your authenticity, vulnerability, and transparency in sharing your story will not only inspire your team and colleagues but also resonate deeply with your customers and clients. It builds trust, fosters connection, and solidifies your leadership position. Think of it as a powerful form of marketing, not in the traditional sense of advertising, but in the authentic expression of your faith journey and its impact on your business.

The key is to frame your story not just as a recounting of hardship, but as a testament to God's faithfulness. Focus on the moments of doubt, despair, and defeat, but more importantly, on the moments of divine intervention, miraculous breakthroughs, and unwavering faith that led to your ultimate triumph. Emphasize the lessons learned, the growth experienced, and the enduring strength that emerged from the crucible of your challenges.

This is not about glorifying the pain; it's about glorifying God's grace in overcoming the pain. The narrative arc of your testimony should showcase God's hand in your life, revealing His faithfulness, His provision, and His unfailing love throughout your journey.

Highlight specific instances where God intervened, answered prayer, or provided unexpected breakthroughs, demonstrating His active role in your transformation.

Before you share your testimony, take time to carefully craft your narrative. Start with a compelling opening that immediately grabs the audience's attention. This might be a poignant anecdote, a striking statistic, or a powerful question that challenges their assumptions. Develop your story chronologically, highlighting key turning points and significant moments of transformation. Use vivid language and imagery to paint a clear picture of your experiences, both the difficult and the triumphant.

Ensure your delivery matches the power of your story. Practice your speech beforehand, paying attention to your tone, pacing, and body language. A passionate, authentic delivery is crucial for conveying the sincerity and impact of your message. Maintain eye contact with your audience, connecting with them on a personal level. Let your emotions flow naturally, allowing your passion for God and your dedication to His purpose to shine through.

When sharing your vulnerabilities, do so with grace and dignity. Avoid dwelling on self-pity or negativity. Instead, focus on the lessons learned, the strength gained, and the hope that emerged from your struggles. Your honesty and transparency will resonate deeply with the audience, forging a genuine connection and fostering a sense of trust and empathy.

Throughout your narrative, weave in scriptural references and faith-based insights that illuminate the transformative power of God. These scriptural anchors will ground your story in spiritual truth, adding depth and meaning to your message. For instance, if you overcame a period of financial hardship, you could reference verses on provision and abundance. If you faced betrayal, you could share verses on forgiveness and grace. Integrating scriptures organically will enhance the spiritual resonance of your testimony.

Consider the specific audience you're addressing. Tailor your message to their needs and interests. If you're speaking to entrepreneurs, highlight the business lessons learned from your experiences. If you're addressing a faith-based group, focus on the spiritual growth and transformation you've experienced. By customizing your message, you increase its impact and relevance, connecting with the audience on a deeper level.

After sharing your story, leave the audience with a call to action. Encourage them to reflect on their own lives, identifying areas where God may be calling them to step into their purpose. Offer practical steps they can take to overcome their own challenges, drawing inspiration from your experiences. This could involve prayer, journaling, seeking mentorship, or joining a support group. Ending with a call to action empowers your audience to take ownership of their journeys, transforming inspiration into action.

Remember, sharing your testimony isn't just about telling your story; it's about offering hope and encouragement to others. It's about reminding them that they are not alone in their struggles and that God's grace is sufficient to overcome any obstacle. Your vulnerability can become their strength, your transformation their inspiration. As you share your journey, you'll not only inspire others but also deepen your own faith and understanding of God's transformative power.

Sharing your testimony can take various forms. It could be a formal speech at a conference, a casual conversation with a colleague, or a heartfelt post on social media. Regardless of the platform, authenticity and vulnerability are key. Let your passion shine through, allowing your story to inspire others to pursue their kingdom-focused goals with courage, faith, and unwavering perseverance.

Consider the impact of your testimony on your kingdom-focused business. It's not just about inspiring customers; it's about fostering a culture of faith, resilience, and mutual support within your team. By sharing your story of overcoming adversity, you create a space where vulnerability is valued, mistakes are viewed as opportunities for growth, and faith is the driving force behind all endeavors. This fosters a strong sense of community, strengthens team cohesion, and empowers employees to overcome their own obstacles with faith and courage.

Finally, be prepared for the response. Sharing your vulnerabilities can be emotionally challenging, but it's also incredibly rewarding. You may receive unexpected support, encouragement, and even new opportunities. Embrace the feedback, both positive and negative, as opportunities for continued growth and learning. Remember, God is with you every step of the way, guiding your steps and using your story to transform lives and accelerate His kingdom. Your testimony is not simply a recounting of events; it is a testament to God's power, a beacon of hope for others, and a strategic tool in building a thriving kingdom-focused business that impacts the world. Let your story be a testament to the power of transformation, a testament to the unwavering love and grace of God, and an inspiration to all who hear it.

Turning Challenges into Opportunities for Growth

Let's shift our perspective from viewing challenges as setbacks to considering them as divinely orchestrated opportunities for exponential growth, both spiritually and professionally. This isn't about a Pollyannaish approach to adversity, ignoring the pain and difficulty inherent in trials. It's about a conscious, faith-filled reframing of our mindset, recognizing God's hand even in the midst of the storm. Think of it as a spiritual process, transforming lead into gold, pain into purpose.

Imagine this scenario: Your burgeoning kingdom-focused business, a project birthed in prayer and fueled by faith, encounters a significant obstacle. Perhaps a key partnership collapses, a major client withdraws their contract, or an unexpected economic downturn threatens your stability. The immediate reaction might be panic, fear, and a sense of overwhelming defeat. The temptation to succumb to despair, to question God's plan, is undeniably strong.

But what if we paused, took a deep breath, and viewed this challenge not as a roadblock, but as a detour, a redirection leading to a richer, more fulfilling destination? What if we saw this adversity as a crucible, refining our faith, strengthening our resilience, and revealing hidden strengths we never knew we possessed?

This reframing begins with a conscious act of faith. It requires trusting that God, in His infinite wisdom and love, is orchestrating this seemingly negative event for our ultimate good. This isn't about blind optimism; it's about a deep-seated conviction that God's plan is perfect, even when the circumstances appear chaotic and unpredictable.

Romans 8:28 (KJV) powerfully states, "And we know that all things work together for good to them that love God, to them who are the called according to his purpose." This verse is not a promise of a life devoid of hardship, but a guarantee that even in the face of adversity, God is working behind the scenes, shaping us, molding us, and preparing us for something greater.

The key is to actively seek God's guidance during these challenging times. Engage in fervent prayer, seeking His wisdom, His strength, and His direction. Journal your thoughts and feelings, allowing yourself to process the emotions without judgment. This isn't a time for self-recrimination or wallowing in self-pity; it's a time for honest introspection, seeking God's perspective on the situation.

Often, challenges reveal areas needing improvement within our businesses. Perhaps the failed partnership exposed a weakness in our contracts, our marketing strategy, or our communication skills. The withdrawn client might highlight a gap in our understanding of their needs or a deficiency in our service delivery. The economic downturn could underscore the need for greater financial prudence and diversification.

Instead of allowing these challenges to paralyze us, let's view them as valuable feedback, opportunities for growth and improvement. Let's analyze the situation dispassionately, identifying the root causes of the failure and formulating effective solutions. This process might involve seeking mentorship, consulting with industry experts, or participating in relevant professional development courses.

This is where our faith intersects with practical business acumen. It's not enough to simply pray for a miracle; we need to actively engage in the process of problem-solving, utilizing our skills and resources to address the challenges head-on. This combination of faith and action is what empowers us to transform challenges into opportunities.

This process also strengthens our reliance on God. We realize our limitations and the utter dependence we have on divine intervention. Our humility grows, allowing for deeper spiritual growth and a more profound appreciation of God's role in our lives. This humble stance before God also allows Him to work more freely, inspiring creative solutions that we would never have conceived of on our own.

Consider seeking wise counsel from mentors or advisors experienced in navigating similar business challenges. Their insights and guidance can provide invaluable perspective, offering practical strategies to overcome obstacles and develop innovative solutions. Remember, the wisdom of others, combined with God's guidance, can lead to effective strategies beyond what we could accomplish individually.

In addition to seeking external support, fostering a strong support network within your team is critical. Sharing your challenges with trusted colleagues, creating a space where vulnerability is encouraged, and fostering a collaborative environment of problem-solving can significantly strengthen resilience and enhance team cohesion. This team spirit will prove invaluable in navigating future obstacles.

Furthermore, use this challenge as an opportunity to refine your communication strategies. Reach out to your stakeholders, honestly explaining the situation and outlining your plan for addressing it. Transparency and open communication can build trust, demonstrating your commitment to your clients and solidifying your relationships. The way you navigate the crisis can build stronger bonds.

Remember, the challenges you face today are not intended to define you but to refine you. They are opportunities to demonstrate your faith, your resilience, and your ability to rise above adversity. Each challenge presents a chance to draw closer to God, to strengthen your faith, and to build a more robust and resilient kingdom-focused business. It is through these trials that we are forged into the people God intends us to be, equipped to accomplish the extraordinary purposes He has planned for our lives and businesses. Embrace the challenges, and watch God transform them into extraordinary opportunities.

The journey from pain to purpose isn't a linear path; it's a winding road, full of unexpected turns and unforeseen obstacles. But with faith as our compass and God as our guide, we can navigate any storm and emerge stronger, wiser, and more deeply connected to our divine purpose. The challenges we face are not designed to defeat us, but to refine us, to shape us, to prepare us for the extraordinary things God has planned for our lives and for the kingdom He has called us to build. Each challenge, therefore, is an invitation to grow, to learn, and to draw closer to God. Embrace the challenges, for in them lies the path to unparalleled growth and purpose.

This proactive response to adversity will not only strengthen your business but will also profoundly impact your spiritual growth. The experience will reshape your faith, deepen your trust in God, and expand your capacity for empathy and compassion. The trials you face will help you empathize with the challenges faced by others, enabling you to better serve those within your community and those you serve through your business.

Remember the power of testimony. Your story of overcoming adversity, of transforming pain into purpose, will serve as a beacon of hope and inspiration to others. By sharing your experiences, you will not only help others navigate their own challenges but will also strengthen your own resolve and deepen your faith. Your journey, shared authentically, can become a powerful tool in building a thriving kingdom-focused business and expanding God's influence in the world. Let your experiences be a testament to God's faithfulness and a catalyst for inspiring others to pursue their own kingdom purposes.

The process of transforming challenges into opportunities is an ongoing journey, not a destination. It requires continuous self-reflection, prayerful discernment, and a willingness to learn from every experience, both positive and negative. It's a journey of faith, perseverance, and unwavering trust in God's plan, even when the path ahead seems uncertain. Embrace the challenges, for within them lies the potential for extraordinary growth, both spiritually and professionally, a testament to the transformative power of God's grace. The difficulties you overcome become stepping stones on your path towards the abundant life God promises.

Finding Purpose in Suffering

Let's explore the profound power of empathy and community in navigating life's inevitable trials. We've established the principle of transforming pain into purpose, of viewing challenges as opportunities for growth. But the journey isn't always solitary. In fact, some of the most significant breakthroughs occur within the context of shared experience, mutual support, and the collective strength of a faith-based community.

Imagine a support group, a gathering of individuals facing similar challenges. Perhaps they're entrepreneurs navigating the turbulent waters of a competitive market, struggling with cash flow, facing unforeseen setbacks, or grappling with the emotional weight of business failures. Perhaps they are individuals dealing with personal loss, health crises, or family difficulties that significantly impact their spiritual and professional lives. Each person carries a unique story, a personal narrative etched with pain, frustration, and uncertainty.

Yet, within this shared space, a remarkable transformation begins. As individuals share their vulnerabilities, their struggles, and their triumphs, a powerful sense of unity emerges. The isolation that often accompanies adversity dissolves, replaced by a profound sense of connection and belonging. Hearing others' stories – tales of hardship and resilience – offers a powerful validation of personal experiences. It's in this space of shared vulnerability that a sense of belonging and hope can begin to bloom.

The beauty of a faith-based support group lies in its grounding in the unwavering love and grace of God. Within this environment, individuals are not only encouraged to share their experiences but also to lean on the collective wisdom and faith of the community. Prayers are shared, scriptures are read, and testimonies of God's faithfulness are exchanged, providing comfort, hope, and encouragement.

This isn't simply about offering platitudes or providing superficial solutions. It's about creating a space where raw emotions can be processed honestly and openly, where individuals feel safe to express their pain without judgment or condemnation. It's about embracing the messy reality of life, recognizing that faith doesn't negate suffering but rather provides a framework for navigating it with strength, grace, and unwavering hope.

Consider the power of shared prayer. When individuals come together to pray for one another, a collective energy of faith is unleashed. This unified petition isn't simply a symbolic act; it's a tangible demonstration of God's power to heal, restore, and provide strength. This collective effort fosters a sense of shared destiny and reinforces that struggles are shared rather than isolating experiences. It is a powerful tool in the process of transforming pain into purpose.

Active listening plays a crucial role in this community-building process. It's not enough to simply hear another person's story; we must listen with empathy, seeking to understand their perspective, their pain, and their hopes. This involves setting aside our own judgments and preconceived notions, creating a safe space where individuals feel truly heard and understood.

This active listening strengthens empathy, a critical skill for anyone seeking to build thriving relationships, both personal and professional. Empathy allows us to step into another person's shoes, to experience their pain as if it were our own. This understanding not only deepens our compassion but also helps us develop more effective strategies for supporting those around us.

Building empathy requires mindful practice. It's about paying attention to nonverbal cues, observing body language, and actively listening to the emotions expressed in someone's voice. It also means asking clarifying questions, seeking to understand the nuances of their experiences, and avoiding interrupting or offering unsolicited advice. Authentic empathy requires time, patience, and a genuine desire to connect with others on a deeper level.

In addition to actively listening, offering practical support is essential. This might involve connecting individuals with relevant resources, offering assistance with daily tasks, or simply providing a listening ear. The practical support, coupled with emotional support, builds mutual respect and trust, reinforcing the strength of community and solidarity. Remember, faith is not simply a belief system; it's a way of life that compels us to act on our beliefs.

Beyond the immediate support offered within a community setting, consider the power of mentorship. Experienced individuals who have successfully navigated similar challenges can offer invaluable guidance, providing both practical strategies and spiritual encouragement. Mentoring relationships are crucial for personal and professional growth, especially when navigating the complexities of business and life's challenges.

Mentorship goes beyond offering simple advice. It's about establishing a long-term relationship based on mutual respect, trust, and a shared commitment to growth. It's a journey of learning, where both mentor and mentee grow and benefit from the relationship. Mentors can provide crucial emotional support, a critical aspect often overlooked in traditional business settings.

This mentoring relationship, built upon Christian principles, emphasizes faith, perseverance, and resilience. It's an opportunity to not just share practical business knowledge but also to support spiritual growth and cultivate a strong sense of community. It reinforces the idea that success is not solely measured by financial gains but also by spiritual maturity and a commitment to service.

As you engage in these acts of service and community building, remember the transformative power of forgiveness. Holding onto resentment or bitterness only perpetuates pain and hinders our ability to move forward. Forgiveness, both of ourselves and of others, is an essential step in the healing process. It's a conscious decision to release the burden of negativity, allowing ourselves to experience the freedom and peace that comes with grace.

Forgiveness is not condoning harmful actions; it's about releasing the emotional weight of pain, making space for healing and growth. It's a journey of releasing control, allowing God to restore the broken pieces and bring about reconciliation and healing. It's an act that strengthens our spiritual resilience and allows us to fully embrace the transformative power of God's grace.

Finally, remember the importance of celebrating successes, both large and small. Acknowledging milestones, sharing testimonies of God's faithfulness, and celebrating collective victories strengthens community bonds and inspires others to persevere in the face of adversity. Celebrating achievements, whether professional or personal, reinforces the idea that setbacks are temporary and that, through faith and perseverance, we can overcome any challenge.

The path from pain to purpose is not a solitary journey. It's a collective experience, shared within the context of a loving and supportive community, fortified by faith and fuelled by the power of shared experience. Embrace the power of community, for it is in unity that we find the strength to transform pain into purpose, adversity into opportunity, and ultimately, to build the kingdom of God, one transformed life at a time. The strength of the collective faith will amplify your individual capacity for transformation. The journey will be far more fruitful and fulfilling when undertaken together.

DEVELOPING RESILIENCE AND EMOTIONAL INTELLIGENCE

Building resilience and emotional intelligence is not merely a self-improvement exercise; it's a spiritual discipline that equips us to navigate the inevitable storms of life with grace, wisdom, and unwavering faith. The path from pain to purpose is often paved with conflict – disagreements with colleagues, strained relationships with family, or challenging encounters with clients. These situations, while often unpleasant, present invaluable opportunities for growth and refinement of our character, provided we approach them with the right mindset and tools.

Let's consider a scenario: you're leading a team working on a critical project. Deadlines loom, pressures mount, and a crucial disagreement erupts between two key team members. One member, let's call them 'Sarah', believes a particular approach is best, while 'David' champions an alternative strategy. The tension is palpable; voices are raised; and the air crackles with negativity. This isn't just a professional disagreement; it's a conflict that threatens to derail the project and damage team morale.

In this moment, your emotional intelligence becomes your most valuable asset. Ignoring the conflict, hoping it will just disappear, is not an option. Instead, your faith-based approach will guide you towards a solution that honors both the project's success and the well-being of your team members.

The first step is self-regulation. Before engaging with Sarah and David, take a moment to center yourself. Pray for guidance, seeking wisdom and discernment. Practice deep breathing exercises to calm your nervous system and clear your mind. Remember that your emotional state will significantly influence how you handle the situation. Reacting from a place of anxiety or anger will likely escalate the conflict. Instead, approach the situation with a heart of compassion and a commitment to understanding.

Next, focus on empathy. Actively listen to both Sarah and David, seeking to understand their perspectives without judgment. Try to see the situation from each individual's point of view. What are their underlying concerns? What are their unmet needs? Why are they so passionate about their respective strategies? Empathy requires stepping outside your own perspective and embracing their emotions as if they were your own. This isn't about agreeing with them, but about truly understanding their emotional experience. Ask clarifying questions to ensure a clear understanding of their motivations. For example, you might ask Sarah, "Sarah, I understand you feel strongly about this approach. Can you help me understand why it's so important to you?" Similarly, with David, "David, I hear your concerns. Can you elaborate on why you think your strategy is better suited for this situation?"

Active listening is more than simply hearing words; it's about observing body language, tone of voice, and nonverbal cues. It's about giving your full attention and creating a safe space where both individuals feel heard and respected. Remember the power of silence; allow space for reflection and processing. Avoid interrupting or offering unsolicited advice before fully understanding their positions. This respectful listening is a powerful tool in de-escalating conflict and building bridges of understanding. This process requires patience, a willingness to listen beyond what is explicitly stated, and a genuine desire to understand their perspective. The goal isn't to win the argument; it's to find a solution that honors everyone's concerns.

Once you've fully understood both perspectives, you can begin to facilitate a constructive dialogue. Encourage Sarah and David to express their concerns openly and honestly, but in a respectful manner. Guide the conversation towards finding common ground. Are there elements of both strategies that could be combined? Are there alternative solutions that would address the concerns of both individuals? This process necessitates patience and a commitment to collaborative problem-solving. It might require multiple conversations, periods of reflection, and a willingness to compromise. Remember that conflict resolution isn't about winning, but about finding a solution that benefits the entire team. This might involve suggesting a compromise, identifying areas of mutual agreement, or seeking outside expertise to mediate.

Throughout the process, maintain a spirit of humility and grace. Acknowledge your own limitations and biases. Be willing to admit when you've made a mistake. Model the behavior you wish to see in others – respect, empathy, and a willingness to collaborate. Your actions will speak louder than words, influencing the team's overall response to the conflict. This is also an excellent opportunity to instill the importance of forgiveness within the team dynamic. If harsh words were exchanged, create space for reconciliation and forgiveness, modeling the healing power of Christ-like love.

This situation illustrates the importance of emotional intelligence in navigating conflicts. It's about managing your own emotions, understanding the emotions of others, and using this understanding to build bridges, resolve disagreements, and foster stronger relationships. This is not simply a professional skill; it's a spiritual discipline. By incorporating faith-based principles of empathy, forgiveness, and humility, you can transform challenging situations into opportunities for growth, strengthening your resilience and deepening your relationships. The Bible repeatedly underscores the importance of love, understanding, and forgiveness in resolving conflicts (Matthew 5:23-24; Ephesians 4:2-3; Colossians 3:12-15). These are not just suggestions; they are spiritual tools to navigate challenges.

Beyond this specific scenario, let's consider the broader development of resilience and emotional intelligence. These aren't innate qualities; they are skills that can be cultivated through conscious effort and mindful practice. Consider incorporating daily practices like mindfulness meditation, journaling, and prayer to enhance your self-awareness and emotional regulation. Mindfulness allows you to observe your emotions without judgment, providing a space to recognize patterns, triggers, and responses. Journaling provides an avenue to process your emotions and reflect on your experiences. Through these practices, you gain insight into your strengths and weaknesses, equipping you to respond more effectively to challenging situations.

Further, cultivate a growth mindset. View challenges not as insurmountable obstacles but as opportunities for learning and growth. Embrace setbacks as learning experiences, analyzing what went wrong and identifying strategies for future success. This shift in perspective transforms adversity into a catalyst for personal and spiritual growth. This mindset also requires a level of self-compassion. Be kind to yourself, acknowledging your limitations while celebrating your strengths. Avoid self-criticism; focus instead on self-improvement.

Surrounding yourself with a supportive community is also critical. Share your challenges with trusted mentors, friends, or family members. Their encouragement, advice, and prayers can provide strength during difficult times. The support of a faith-based community offers a network of spiritual support, accountability, and encouragement. This network reinforces your resolve, providing a sense of belonging and shared purpose.

Building resilience and emotional intelligence is a journey, not a destination. It requires continuous learning, self-reflection, and a commitment to personal growth. By integrating faith-based principles into your approach, you not only develop crucial life skills but also deepen your relationship with God, transforming pain into purpose and building a life of meaning and significance. This transformation isn't just about surviving; it's about thriving amidst adversity, drawing strength from your faith and your ever-expanding emotional intelligence. Remember, your faith is not a passive belief system; it's an active force that empowers you to navigate the complexities of life with unwavering hope and resilience.

CHAPTER 4

Cultivating Kingdom Confidence

UNDERSTANDING YOUR IDENTITY IN CHRIST

Understanding your inherent worth isn't about achieving external validation; it's about recognizing the intrinsic value God has placed within you. This deep-seated confidence, rooted in your identity as a child of God, is the bedrock of Kingdom confidence. It's the unshakeable belief in who you are, not based on your accomplishments or failures, but on the unwavering love and acceptance of your Heavenly Father. This is a profoundly transformative understanding, one that liberates you from the constant need for external approval and empowers you to face life's challenges with resilience and unwavering faith.

This journey of self-discovery begins with a fundamental truth: you are fearfully and wonderfully made (Psalm 139:14). This isn't a mere poetic statement; it's a divine declaration of your unique and invaluable worth. God didn't create you by accident; He meticulously crafted you, with specific gifts, talents, and purposes in mind. Your existence isn't a coincidence; it's a testament to His divine plan and a reflection of His boundless love. Embrace this truth. Meditate on it.

Let it sink deep into your heart and mind. This understanding is the cornerstone upon which Kingdom confidence is built.

Often, our sense of self-worth is tied to external factors – our achievements, our possessions, our social standing. We base our value on what others think of us, allowing their opinions to dictate our self-perception. This creates a precarious foundation for our confidence, one that crumbles easily under the weight of criticism or failure. Kingdom confidence, however, stands firm amidst the storms of life because it's anchored in an immutable truth: God's unconditional love.

Imagine a precious gemstone, perfectly formed and exquisitely beautiful. It's worth isn't determined by its setting or whether it's displayed in a museum or tucked away in a drawer. Its inherent value remains constant, regardless of its surroundings. You are that gemstone – precious, valuable, and loved unconditionally by your Creator. Your worth is intrinsic; it's not something you need to earn or prove. This understanding releases you from the relentless pursuit of external validation.

The process of uncovering your identity in Christ is a personal journey, a process of peeling back the layers of self-doubt and societal conditioning to reveal the radiant beauty within. It requires introspection, prayer, and a willingness to embrace God's truth. Begin by spending time in quiet reflection, asking God to reveal your unique gifts and purposes. Journal your thoughts and feelings, allowing yourself to explore your deepest beliefs about your worth. What messages have you internalized from your upbringing, your relationships, and your experiences? Are these messages aligned with God's truth?

Consider engaging in spiritual practices that deepen your connection with God. Regular prayer, Bible study, and meditation can nurture your faith and illuminate your identity as a child of God. Immerse yourself in scripture, allowing God's word to penetrate your soul and transform your perspective. Read passages that emphasize God's love, acceptance, and forgiveness. Let these scriptures become affirmations, internalizing their truth and believing them in your heart.

Engage in active listening during prayer. Don't just ask God to reveal your identity; listen for His response. This may come through scripture, a sermon, a conversation with a trusted friend, or even a quiet whisper in your heart. Be attentive to the subtle ways God communicates with you. It's crucial to discern His voice amidst the noise of life's distractions.

Furthermore, cultivate a practice of gratitude. Take time each day to acknowledge and appreciate the blessings in your life, both big and small. This practice shifts your focus from your shortcomings to God's abundant provision. It reinforces your sense of worth, reminding you that you are loved and cherished. Gratitude isn't just a feel-good exercise; it's a spiritual discipline that strengthens your faith and enhances your overall well-being.

Another powerful tool in understanding your identity in Christ is forgiveness. Forgive yourself for past mistakes and shortcomings. God's grace is boundless, and His forgiveness extends to every aspect of your life. Holding onto guilt and self-condemnation only hinders your growth and prevents you from fully embracing your identity as a child of God. Release the weight of your past and step into the freedom that comes with God's unconditional love and forgiveness.

Similarly, forgive others who have hurt or wronged you. Holding onto resentment and bitterness prevents you from experiencing the peace and joy that comes with a life surrendered to God. Forgiveness isn't about condoning their actions; it's about releasing yourself from the bondage of anger and bitterness. It's an act of releasing the burden of unforgiveness, freeing yourself to embrace His grace and the fullness of life He offers. This act of forgiveness is not only for your own benefit but also reflects the selfless love and compassion of Christ.

Surround yourself with a supportive community of believers. Fellowship with like-minded individuals strengthens your faith and provides a safe space to share your struggles and celebrate your victories. Share your journey of self-discovery with trusted friends, mentors, or family members. Their encouragement and prayers can be invaluable in your quest for Kingdom confidence.

Remember, cultivating Kingdom confidence is a continuous process, not a one-time event. It requires consistent effort, self-reflection, and a steadfast commitment to living a life aligned with God's will. Embrace the challenges and setbacks as opportunities for growth and learning. Don't be discouraged by setbacks; view them as stepping stones on your path to becoming the person God created you to be. Persevere in faith, trusting in God's unwavering love and support, knowing that He is with you every step of the way.

The journey of self-discovery is unique to each individual. There's no single path or formula for uncovering your identity in Christ. However, the principles outlined above offer a starting point, a framework for your personal exploration. Embrace the journey with an open heart, a teachable spirit, and a deep trust in God's unwavering love.

Through consistent effort and prayer, you will uncover the abundant blessings of God's grace and the immeasurable worth He places on you. Embrace this truth; let it transform your perspective, and empower you to live a life of purpose, significance, and unshakeable Kingdom confidence. This isn't just about self-esteem; it's about knowing your identity in Christ, a truth that empowers you to live a life of purpose, boldness, and unwavering faith. Remember, your value isn't defined by your accomplishments or failures but by the love of your Creator. This profound understanding is the foundation upon which a life of Kingdom confidence is built.

This understanding of your identity in Christ is not merely an intellectual exercise; it's a transformative experience that impacts every aspect of your life. It transforms your relationships, your work, and your overall perspective. This deep sense of worth allows you to navigate life's challenges with greater resilience, compassion, and unwavering faith. It liberates you from the need for external validation, empowering you to live authentically and pursue your God-given purpose with confidence and conviction. You become a beacon of hope and inspiration, radiating the love and grace of Christ to those around you.

This newfound confidence isn't arrogance or self-importance; it's a humble recognition of your worth in God's eyes. It allows you to approach life's challenges with boldness, knowing that you are not alone, and that you are equipped to overcome any obstacle with God's strength and guidance. It enables you to extend grace to others, understanding their struggles and offering compassion and support. It inspires you to use your gifts and talents for God's glory, making a positive impact on the world.

The journey to cultivating Kingdom confidence is a lifelong pursuit. It's a journey of continuous self-discovery, spiritual growth, and unwavering faith. As you deepen your relationship with God, your understanding of your identity in Christ will grow, strengthening your confidence and empowering you to live a life of purpose and significance. Embrace this journey; it's a journey worth taking, a journey that leads to a life of unwavering faith, boundless love, and unshakeable Kingdom confidence. Remember, you are loved, you are valued, and you are uniquely created by a loving God. Embrace your identity in Christ, and watch your confidence soar to new heights.

BREAKING FREE FROM LIMITING BELIEFS

Breaking free from the shackles of limiting beliefs is paramount to cultivating Kingdom confidence. These beliefs, often deeply ingrained from childhood experiences, societal pressures, or past failures, act as invisible barriers, hindering our progress and preventing us from embracing our God-given potential. They whisper doubts, fueling fear and uncertainty, and preventing us from stepping into the fullness of who God created us to be. They are insidious, often operating below the level of conscious awareness, yet wielding significant power over our thoughts, actions, and ultimately, our destiny.

The first step in breaking free is identification. Take time for honest self-reflection, prayerfully examining the narratives you've accepted as truth. What negative messages have you internalized? Do you believe you are unworthy, incapable, or undeserving of success? Do you consistently downplay your accomplishments or focus solely on your failures? Do you struggle with feelings of inadequacy or self-doubt? These questions, when answered honestly and prayerfully, can begin to unearth the root of your limiting beliefs. Journaling can be an invaluable tool in this process, allowing you to articulate your thoughts and feelings without judgment. Write down the specific beliefs that hold you back, acknowledging their impact on your life. This process of bringing these beliefs into the light is the first step toward dismantling their power.

Once you've identified these limiting beliefs, it's crucial to challenge their validity in the light of God's word. Are these beliefs rooted in truth, or are they based on lies and misconceptions? The Bible offers abundant reassurance of God's unconditional love, grace, and acceptance. Scripture is filled with promises of strength, courage, and provision. Compare the negative messages you've internalized with the truth of God's word. For example, if you believe you are unworthy, counter this with scriptures like Psalm 139:14 (KJV), which declares, "I will praise thee; for I am fearfully and wonderfully made: marvellous are thy works; and that my soul knoweth right well" This verse emphasizes your unique and intentional creation, highlighting your inherent worth as a child of God. Similarly, if you believe you are incapable of success, counter this with Philippians 4:13 (KJV): "I can do all things through Christ which strengtheneth me." This verse assures you of God's empowering presence, enabling you to overcome any obstacle.

Remember, engaging in spiritual warfare is not optional; it's essential for overcoming these limiting beliefs. These beliefs are not merely thoughts; they are spiritual strongholds that need to be confronted and dismantled through prayer and the authority given to us in Christ. Engage in fervent prayer, asking God to expose and break the chains of these negative thought patterns. Claim the promises of God's word, declaring them over your life with faith and conviction. Speak truth into your circumstances, replacing lies with God's truth. Declare your identity in Christ, emphasizing your worth, your capabilities, and your divine purpose.

Beyond prayer and scripture, practical steps are essential to reinforce your new positive beliefs. One powerful tool is affirmation. Affirmations are positive statements repeated regularly, reinforcing new, empowering beliefs. Create affirmations based on the truths revealed through your self-reflection and scripture study. For example, if you struggle with self-doubt, an affirmation might be: "I am confident in my abilities, because God has gifted me with unique talents and strengths." Repeat this affirmation daily, visualizing yourself embodying these qualities. This deliberate act of speaking truth over your life, consistently reinforcing positive beliefs, helps to reprogram your subconscious mind.

Another powerful technique is visualization. Spend time each day visualizing yourself achieving your goals and overcoming obstacles. See yourself succeeding in your endeavors, feeling the joy and fulfillment that comes from living a life aligned with God's purpose. This practice strengthens your faith and reinforces your belief in your capabilities. Visualizing success isn't mere wishful thinking; it's a powerful spiritual discipline that aligns your mind with God's will and prepares you to overcome challenges. This act of visualization, when combined with prayer and affirmation, creates a powerful synergy for breaking free from limiting beliefs.

Surrounding yourself with a supportive community is vital in this process. Share your struggles and victories with trusted friends, family, or mentors who can offer encouragement, accountability, and prayer. Find a community where you feel safe to be vulnerable, where you can share your doubts and fears without judgment. The support and fellowship of like-minded believers can be incredibly powerful, helping to reinforce your new positive beliefs and provide strength during challenging times. This support network isn't just emotional; it's a spiritual bulwark against the negativity that fuels limiting beliefs.

Remember, overcoming limiting beliefs is a journey, not a destination. There will be setbacks and challenges along the way. Don't be discouraged by these obstacles; view them as opportunities for growth and learning. As you consistently apply these techniques, you will notice a gradual shift in your mindset, a growing confidence in your abilities, and an increased sense of purpose and fulfillment.

The process of overcoming limiting beliefs is also deeply intertwined with practicing forgiveness. Forgive yourself for past mistakes and shortcomings. God's grace is abundant, and His forgiveness is complete. Holding onto guilt and self-condemnation only reinforces negative beliefs. Release the weight of your past and embrace God's unconditional love and forgiveness. This forgiveness extends to others as well. Release resentment and bitterness, understanding that unforgiveness binds you to negativity and hinders your growth. Forgiveness isn't condoning harmful behavior, but rather releasing the emotional burden that limits your progress. It's a critical component of breaking free from the constraints of limiting beliefs, allowing you to move forward with renewed freedom and confidence.

Furthermore, cultivate a deep sense of gratitude. Take time each day to appreciate the blessings in your life, focusing on God's goodness and provision. Gratitude shifts your perspective, reminding you of God's abundant grace and your inherent worth. This isn't merely a feel-good exercise; it's a spiritual discipline that strengthens your faith and promotes healing. It's a potent antidote to negativity, replacing limiting beliefs with a sense of appreciation and abundance.

Finally, remember the importance of self-care in this process. Prioritize rest, healthy eating, and exercise. Engage in activities that bring you joy and peace. Taking care of your physical and emotional well-being supports your spiritual growth and strengthens your ability to overcome challenges. Neglecting self-care can deplete your energy and resilience, making it harder to combat limiting beliefs. It's an essential element in cultivating Kingdom confidence, ensuring you have the physical and emotional strength needed to face the obstacles ahead.

Breaking free from limiting beliefs is a spiritual battle that requires consistent effort, unwavering faith, and a commitment to living a life aligned with God's will. Embrace the journey with patience, persistence, and a deep trust in God's unwavering love and support. The rewards are immeasurable—a life of purpose, significance, and unshakeable Kingdom confidence. You are fearfully and wonderfully made, uniquely equipped to fulfill God's purpose for your life. Believe it, embrace it, and watch your life transform as you break free from the limitations of negative thinking and step into the abundant life God has prepared for you. Remember, you are a child of the King, and you possess the strength and resources to overcome any challenge.

BUILDING SELF-ESTEEM THROUGH SPIRITUAL PRACTICES

Building a strong sense of self-worth is a cornerstone of Kingdom confidence. While overcoming limiting beliefs forms a crucial foundation, we now delve into the powerful role spiritual practices play in nurturing and elevating self-esteem. These practices aren't mere religious exercises; they are vital tools for transforming our inner landscape, fostering a deep-seated confidence rooted in our identity as beloved children of God.

Prayer, often misunderstood as simply asking for things, is a powerful two-way communication with the Divine. It's a conversation where we pour out our hearts, acknowledging our vulnerabilities, and simultaneously receive strength, comfort, and guidance. Regular, heartfelt prayer helps us connect with a source of unconditional love and acceptance, a love that transcends our perceived flaws and shortcomings. When we consistently communicate with God, acknowledging our dependence on Him, we begin to recognize our inherent worth as His cherished creation.

Consider the practice of "gratitude prayer." Instead of focusing on what we lack, we actively express thankfulness for the blessings in our lives, both big and small. This simple act shifts our perspective, focusing our attention on God's goodness and provision. It helps us recognize the abundance surrounding us, fostering a sense of security and contentment that naturally elevates self-esteem. Start small. Thank God for the warmth of the sun on your face, the food on your table, the roof over your head. Gradually, as you practice this daily, your awareness of God's blessings will expand, leading to a deeper appreciation of your own value within His grand design.

Beyond gratitude, we can utilize prayer for specific areas where self-esteem is lacking. If you struggle with feelings of inadequacy, pray for strength and courage, asking God to reveal your hidden talents and abilities. If you grapple with self-doubt, pray for clarity and discernment, asking God to guide your decisions and reassure you of His unwavering support. Prayer isn't an unknown act, but a powerful tool that connects us to a boundless source of strength and guidance, empowering us to overcome self-limiting beliefs and embrace our God-given potential.

Meditation, often associated with Eastern traditions, finds a rich place within the Christian faith as a means of centering ourselves in God's presence. It's not about emptying our minds, but about focusing our thoughts on God, allowing His peace and love to permeate our being. Regular meditation cultivates a sense of inner calm and reduces stress, which are significant contributors to low self-esteem. When we are stressed and anxious, our self-perception is often skewed, leading to negative self-talk and self-criticism. Meditation acts as an antidote, creating a space for inner stillness and self-compassion.

One effective meditation technique involves focusing on a scripture verse that speaks to your self-worth. Choose a verse that resonates deeply with you, perhaps Psalm 139:14 (KJV) ("I will praise thee; for I am fearfully and wonderfully made: marvellous are thy works; and that my soul knoweth right well."), or Ephesians 2:10 (KJV) ("For we are his workmanship, created in Christ Jesus unto good works, which God hath before ordained that we should walk in them."). Repeat the verse slowly and deliberately, visualizing the meaning behind the words. Allow the truth of the scripture to penetrate your heart and mind, transforming negative self-perception into a confident affirmation of your divine identity.

Another powerful meditation technique involves practicing "centering prayer." This involves choosing a powerful word or phrase, such as "God's love," and silently repeating it throughout your meditation time. As you repeat this phrase, let your attention rest on God's presence within you. When your mind wanders, gently bring your attention back to your chosen phrase and continue the practice. This simple practice helps you to quiet the mental chatter and connect with the source of all peace and love. By regularly practicing centering prayer, you will cultivate a sense of calm and inner stability, which forms a strong foundation for cultivating self-esteem.

Bible study isn't just about acquiring knowledge; it's about engaging in a transformative conversation with God. As we delve into Scripture, we encounter God's unwavering love, His unconditional acceptance, and His unwavering commitment to our growth and well-being. These truths, when internalized, have the power to reshape our self-perception, replacing negative beliefs with a confident affirmation of our identity in Christ.

Choose specific passages that address self-worth and identity. Consider reading Psalms, Proverbs, or the Gospels. Pay close attention to the promises and assurances that God offers. As you read, ask the Holy Spirit to illuminate the meaning and apply it to your life. Reflect on how these truths challenge your negative self-perception and how they can empower you to live a life of greater confidence. Journaling your reflections can further deepen the impact of your Bible study, providing space to process the insights you gain and apply them to your everyday life.

Beyond focused reading, consider thematic study. For instance, explore the theme of God's love in the Bible. Read passages that describe God's love for His people, His forgiveness of their sins, and His relentless pursuit of their well-being. As you immerse yourself in this theme, allow yourself to experience the depth and breadth of God's love, which directly addresses the root of low self-esteem: the belief that you are unworthy or unloved. Understanding God's boundless love for you is a critical step toward fostering a healthier self-image.

Incorporating these spiritual practices into your daily routine—consistent prayer, mindful meditation, and intentional Bible study—will profoundly impact your self-esteem. It's not a quick fix, but a gradual transformation of your inner landscape. Be patient with yourself, celebrate small victories, and consistently nurture your connection with God. As you do so, you will discover a deep wellspring of self-worth, unshakeable confidence, and a radiant sense of your identity as a beloved child of the King.

The environment you create for these practices matters. Choose a quiet, peaceful space where you can be undisturbed. It might be a corner of your home, a quiet park bench, or even your car before heading to work. Ensure the space is free from distractions, allowing you to focus fully on your interaction with God. Consider creating a special space with meaningful elements, such as a candle, a piece of artwork, and your cherished Bible. These physical elements can enhance the spiritual atmosphere and create a conducive environment for self-reflection and spiritual growth.

Along with creating a physical space, nurture a mental environment conducive to spiritual growth. Before you begin your prayer, meditation, or Bible study, take a few deep breaths to center yourself and quiet your mind. Let go of worries and anxieties, allowing your focus to shift towards God and His presence in your life. Treat this time as a sacred appointment with God, honoring it with your full attention and intentionality.

Remember that building self-esteem is a process, not a destination. There will be days when you feel more confident than others. There may be times when doubts and insecurities creep in. Be patient with yourself, acknowledging these feelings without judgment. View setbacks as opportunities for growth and learning. Continue to nurture your relationship with God through prayer, meditation, and Bible study, and trust in His unwavering love and support. As you consistently engage in these practices, you will find that your self-esteem gradually strengthens, fostering a deep sense of confidence that is firmly rooted in your identity as a beloved child of God. This unshakeable confidence is the hallmark of Kingdom confidence—a confident assurance grounded in faith, empowering you to live a life of purpose, significance, and abiding joy.

MS. ALISHA JACKSON, MSW

SETTING BOUNDARIES AND PROTECTING YOUR ENERGY

Building unshakeable Kingdom confidence isn't solely about internal work; it necessitates establishing healthy boundaries to protect our precious energy and prevent burnout. Think of your energy as a finite resource, a wellspring of vitality that fuels your spiritual walk, your professional endeavors, and your personal relationships. Just as a wise farmer carefully manages their crops, ensuring they receive adequate sunlight, water, and nutrients, we must be equally diligent in protecting our energy reserves. Without healthy boundaries, we risk depletion, leading to frustration, resentment, and ultimately, hindering our ability to fulfill God's purpose for our lives.

Setting boundaries isn't about being selfish; it's an act of self-preservation, a crucial element of self-care. It's about recognizing our limitations, respecting our needs, and prioritizing our well-being. It's about honoring the sacred temple God has entrusted us with, ensuring it remains a sanctuary of peace and strength. When we fail to set boundaries, we inadvertently invite others to deplete our energy, leaving us feeling drained, overwhelmed, and resentful. This, in turn, negatively impacts our ability to effectively serve God and others.

Let's explore practical strategies for establishing and maintaining healthy boundaries. Remember, setting boundaries is a journey, not a destination. It involves consistent effort, self-awareness, and a willingness to adjust our approach as needed.

In the Workplace:

The professional arena often presents unique challenges to setting boundaries. The pressure to perform, the demands of colleagues, and the ever-present need to prove ourselves can easily lead to overcommitment and burnout. It's crucial to establish clear boundaries that protect our time, energy, and emotional well-being.

One key aspect is managing our workload effectively. Learn to say "no" to additional tasks when your plate is already full. Don't be afraid to politely decline requests that stretch you beyond your capacity or fall outside your defined responsibilities. Remember, saying "no" to one thing opens the door to saying "yes" to something more aligned with your priorities and God's purpose for your life. This isn't about being uncooperative; it's about prioritizing your well-being and maximizing your efficiency.

Effective communication is paramount. Clearly articulate your availability and limitations to your colleagues and supervisors. Communicate your need for breaks, your preferred working hours, and your expectations regarding response times. This proactive communication avoids misunderstandings and ensures that others respect your boundaries.

Establish clear communication channels. Define your preferred method of communication – email, phone, instant messaging – and specify when you are most responsive. This helps prevent constant interruptions and allows you to focus on tasks without being constantly pulled in multiple directions. Avoid the temptation to be constantly "on" – check emails and messages at designated times, rather than allowing them to dictate your schedule. This creates mental space and improves productivity.

Protect your personal time. Avoid working outside of designated hours whenever possible. Respect your weekends and evenings, ensuring that they remain sacred spaces for rest, family time, and spiritual renewal. This separation prevents work from encroaching on personal life and protects your mental health.

In Personal Relationships:

Setting boundaries in personal relationships can be even more challenging, often requiring courage and vulnerability. However, healthy boundaries are vital for nurturing strong, fulfilling relationships built on mutual respect and understanding.

Identify your personal limits. Reflect on the areas where you frequently feel drained or resentful in your relationships. Are you a people-pleaser, often prioritizing others' needs above your own? Do you find yourself constantly giving without receiving in return?

Understanding your limitations is the first step toward setting healthy boundaries.

Communicate your needs assertively yet lovingly. Express your needs clearly and directly, but avoid blame or accusations. Use "I" statements, such as "I need some time alone to recharge," or "I find myself feeling overwhelmed when I'm expected to do everything." The goal is to convey your needs respectfully while ensuring your voice is heard.

Learn to say "no" without guilt. Saying "no" to requests that deplete your energy or compromise your values doesn't mean you don't care; it means you are prioritizing your well-being and setting healthy limits. This requires practice and self-compassion, particularly if you are prone to people-pleasing.

Establish healthy distance when necessary. Recognize that some relationships may require more distance than others. This isn't about cutting people out of your life, but about creating space for your own growth and well-being. It could involve limiting contact with those who consistently drain your energy.

Practice self-compassion. Setting boundaries can be emotionally challenging, especially if you are accustomed to prioritizing others' needs above your own. Be kind to yourself, acknowledge your feelings, and celebrate your progress in establishing healthier boundaries.

Remember that setting boundaries is not about pushing people away; it's about creating space for healthy, reciprocal relationships. When we protect our energy, we can invest more fully in the relationships that truly nourish us, fostering deeper connections and mutual respect.

Spiritual Warfare and Boundary Setting:

Setting boundaries also extends to the spiritual realm. We must be aware of the spiritual forces that seek to undermine our well-being and hinder our progress. Just as we establish physical boundaries, we need to erect spiritual defenses to protect our minds, hearts, and spirits from negativity.

This involves discerning the sources of energy depletion. Are you constantly bombarded by negativity in the media, in your social circles, or even through your own inner dialogue? Identify these sources and consciously limit your exposure.

Engage in spiritual practices that strengthen your spiritual defenses. Prayer, meditation, and Bible study are invaluable tools in fortifying your spirit and resisting negative influences. These practices help you connect with God's power and receive His protection and guidance.

Employ spiritual weapons provided by God's word. The Bible provides various tools for spiritual warfare, such as the Armor of God (Ephesians 6:10-18), which includes the shield of faith and the helmet of salvation. These spiritual weapons protect us against the enemy's schemes and provide strength and courage in facing adversity.

Setting boundaries is an ongoing practice, a continual process of refinement and adjustment. It requires self-awareness, courage, and consistent effort. As we diligently protect our energy reserves, we unlock our full potential, creating space for God's blessings to flow freely into our lives. By creating a life governed by healthy boundaries, we live a life of vibrant Kingdom confidence, able to serve God and others with unwavering passion and unwavering purpose. This isn't simply about personal well-being; it's about maximizing our capacity to impact the world for God's glory. The strength we gain from setting boundaries fuels our mission, allowing us to live lives of significance, influence, and unwavering faith. It allows us to radiate the love of Christ, effectively sharing His message and building His kingdom on earth.

DEVELOPING SELF-COMPASSION AND FORGIVENESS

We've explored the vital role of boundaries in preserving our energy and fostering Kingdom confidence. Now, let's delve into two equally crucial components: self-compassion and forgiveness. These aren't merely feel-good concepts; they are essential pillars supporting our spiritual and professional growth, laying the foundation for unshakeable confidence in our God-given purpose. Without them, the boundaries we've so carefully constructed can become walls, imprisoning us in self-criticism and resentment, hindering our ability to move forward in faith.

Imagine yourself in a quiet space, perhaps a sun-drenched corner of your home, or a peaceful spot in nature. Close your eyes and take a few deep breaths, centering yourself in God's presence. Let the gentle rhythm of your breath wash away the anxieties and self-doubts that may linger. Today, we're embarking on a journey of self-discovery, a pilgrimage into the heart of your being, where self-compassion and forgiveness reside.

Self-compassion, often misunderstood as self-indulgence, is actually an act of radical self-love. It's about treating yourself with the same kindness, understanding, and empathy you would offer a dear friend struggling with similar challenges. It's recognizing your inherent worthiness, regardless of your mistakes or imperfections. We all falter; we all make errors. The key lies in how we respond to these setbacks. Do we succumb to self-criticism and condemnation, or do we embrace self-compassion, acknowledging our humanity while striving for growth?

Let's consider the times you've been hardest on yourself. Perhaps a missed deadline at work, a strained relationship, or a personal failure. Revisit these moments with a renewed perspective. Instead of dwelling on your shortcomings, acknowledge the circumstances, the pressures, and the emotions that contributed to the situation. Recognize that you did the best you could with the resources you had at the time. This isn't about excusing your actions, but about understanding them within a context of human fallibility.

Now, imagine extending the same grace and understanding you've offered yourself to another person struggling with a similar experience. How would you respond? Would you condemn them? Or would you offer words of comfort, empathy, and encouragement? This is the essence of self-compassion. It's about shifting from self-judgment to self-acceptance, recognizing your inherent worthiness and potential for growth.

This isn't a passive acceptance of mediocrity; it's an active embrace of your journey, acknowledging both your strengths and your weaknesses. Self-compassion fuels perseverance. It empowers you to learn from your mistakes, to rise from setbacks, and to continue striving towards your God-given goals. It allows you to approach challenges with a sense of calm resilience, knowing that you are loved, supported, and capable of overcoming obstacles.

This journey of self-compassion is intrinsically linked with forgiveness. Forgiveness isn't merely a Christian virtue; it's a necessity for emotional and spiritual well-being. Holding onto resentment, bitterness, or anger is like carrying a heavy burden, weighing down your spirit and hindering your ability to move forward. Forgiveness, however, is not condoning harmful actions; it's a conscious release of the negativity that binds you.

Begin by forgiving yourself. Let go of the guilt, shame, and self-condemnation that may have accumulated over time. Acknowledge your mistakes, but don't let them define you. Remember that God's love is unconditional, boundless, and ever-present. His forgiveness extends to every aspect of your being, embracing your flaws and celebrating your potential. Embrace His grace and allow it to wash over you, cleansing your heart and mind.

Next, extend that forgiveness to others. This can be the most challenging aspect, particularly when dealing with deeply hurtful experiences. However, the process of forgiveness is not primarily for the benefit of the person who wronged you; it's for your own liberation. Holding onto resentment only serves to keep you tethered to the past, preventing you from embracing the present and building a brighter future.

Forgiveness doesn't mean forgetting; it means choosing to release the negativity, the pain, and the resentment that bind you. It's a conscious decision to let go, to break free from the shackles of the past and step into the freedom of God's grace. It may require time, patience, and even professional guidance, but the rewards are immeasurable.

Consider using prayer as a powerful tool in both self-forgiveness and forgiving others. Pray for understanding, for clarity, and for the strength to let go of the negativity that weighs you down. Pray for the individuals you need to forgive, asking God to soften your heart and grant you the compassion to release the burden of resentment.

This process of self-compassion and forgiveness isn't a one-time event; it's an ongoing practice, a continuous journey of self-discovery and spiritual growth. It requires consistent effort, self-awareness, and a willingness to embrace vulnerability. It's about recognizing your humanity, acknowledging your imperfections, and extending grace to yourself and others. It's about living in the light of God's unconditional love, allowing His grace to transform your heart and empower you to live a life of unwavering Kingdom confidence.

As you cultivate self-compassion and forgiveness, you will find that your capacity for love, empathy, and understanding will expand. You will become more resilient, better equipped to navigate the challenges of life, and more empowered to pursue your God-given purpose. The walls that may have once seemed insurmountable will begin to crumble, replaced by open doors leading to a future filled with hope, purpose, and unwavering Kingdom confidence.

Remember the declarations, affirmations, and prayers we explored in previous chapters. Incorporate these practices into your daily routine, especially when you feel the weight of self-criticism or resentment. Repeat affirmations that emphasize your worthiness, your capabilities, and God's unwavering love. Engage in regular prayer, seeking guidance, strength, and healing. Journal your thoughts and feelings, allowing yourself to process your emotions in a safe and constructive manner.

Cultivating self-compassion and forgiveness is a vital step in building unshakeable Kingdom confidence. It's a journey of self-discovery, a pilgrimage into the heart of your being, where you'll uncover the strength, resilience, and unwavering faith that reside within. It's an act of radical self-love, an embrace of your humanity, and a recognition of your inherent worthiness in God's eyes. As you embark on this journey, remember that you are not alone. God is with you, every step of the way, guiding, supporting, and empowering you to achieve His perfect will for your life. Embrace this journey with courage, faith, and unwavering belief in your potential. The Kingdom of God awaits your full participation, and self-compassion and forgiveness unlock the doors to that participation. They are not merely spiritual exercises; they are foundational elements in building a life of purpose, impact, and abiding joy. Allow God to work within you, transforming your heart and empowering you to radiate His love to the world around you.

Let's take a moment now for quiet reflection. Close your eyes, take a deep breath, and reflect on the lessons we've discussed. Allow yourself to feel the presence of God's love and grace. Embrace the journey of self-compassion and forgiveness, knowing that it is a path towards greater freedom, fulfillment, and Kingdom confidence. May God bless your journey.

CHAPTER 5

Building a Thriving Kingdom Community

THE IMPORTANCE OF MENTORSHIP AND ACCOUNTABILITY

Having established the bedrock of self-compassion and forgiveness as essential elements for building Kingdom confidence, we now turn our attention to the power of community and the vital roles mentorship and accountability play in accelerating our spiritual and professional growth. These aren't optional extras; they are integral components in the construction of a thriving, Kingdom-focused life and business. Think of them as the scaffolding that supports the structure, enabling it to reach its full potential and withstand the inevitable storms that life throws our way.

Mentorship, at its core, is a divinely ordained partnership designed for mutual growth and encouragement. It's a relationship where a more experienced individual, the mentor, guides and supports a less experienced person, the mentee, helping them navigate the complexities of life and business. This isn't about one person holding all the answers; it's about a synergistic exchange of knowledge, experience, and wisdom, all guided by the Holy Spirit. The mentor shares their insights, challenges, and successes, providing invaluable lessons learned that the mentee can use to avoid pitfalls and accelerate their journey. In return, the mentee offers fresh perspectives, enthusiasm, and a willingness to learn, potentially even inspiring the mentor to revisit their own goals and perspectives. It's a beautifully symbiotic relationship, where both individuals are blessed and challenged to grow.

Consider the biblical example of Elijah and Elisha. Elijah, a seasoned prophet, took Elisha under his wing, mentoring him and passing on the mantle of leadership. Elisha learned not only prophetic skills but also the importance of unwavering faith and obedience to God's calling. Their relationship wasn't transactional; it was a deep, spiritual connection built on mutual respect, trust, and a shared commitment to God's purpose. This partnership empowered Elisha to become one of the most impactful prophets in Israel's history. Their story serves as a powerful testament to the transformative power of mentorship.

The benefits of mentorship are multifold. For the mentor, it's an opportunity to use their gifts and experience to bless others, enriching their own spiritual life in the process. The act of sharing wisdom and guiding others strengthens their own understanding and deepens their faith. It's a fulfilling expression of their calling, a chance to leave a lasting legacy. For the mentee, the rewards are equally substantial. Mentorship provides access to knowledge, wisdom, and support that would otherwise be unavailable. A mentor can offer guidance on navigating difficult decisions, overcoming obstacles, and staying focused on God's plan. This support system can be invaluable during challenging times, providing encouragement and accountability. Furthermore, a mentor can help the mentee identify and develop their spiritual gifts, guiding them toward their God-given purpose.

Think of a young entrepreneur launching a Kingdom-focused business. A seasoned mentor, with experience in business and faith, can offer invaluable guidance on navigating the challenges of starting and growing a business while staying true to their faith. They can provide insights into marketing, finance, and leadership, sharing practical strategies learned through years of experience. Crucially, they can also help the mentee maintain spiritual integrity throughout the process, ensuring their business aligns with God's values and principles. This guidance can save the mentee years of struggle, allowing them to accelerate their growth and impact.

But mentorship isn't just a one-way street. It's a dynamic, evolving relationship requiring mutual commitment and effort. Both the mentor and mentee need to be willing to invest time, energy, and emotional vulnerability into the relationship. Regular communication, open dialogue, and a willingness to receive and offer constructive feedback are all essential elements. Effective mentorship requires both parties to be proactive, setting clear goals, expectations, and a timeline for the relationship. It is also vital to establish a framework for accountability to ensure that the goals are met.

In addition to one-on-one mentorship, group coaching and accountability partnerships offer equally powerful ways to foster growth and support. Group coaching allows individuals to learn from each other's experiences, creating a collaborative learning environment where everyone benefits from the collective wisdom of the group. This shared experience fosters a sense of community and belonging, providing emotional support and encouragement. It's also an excellent platform for holding one another accountable for personal and professional goals.

Accountability partnerships are similar in nature, focusing on creating a structure for mutual support and encouragement. These partnerships, ideally with individuals who share similar faith and goals, provide a safe space to share successes, challenges, and areas needing improvement. The structure of regularly scheduled check-ins and progress reports helps keep both individuals focused on their goals and provides ongoing support when challenges arise. Remember, community is crucial; it acts as a buffer against the isolation that can often hinder our spiritual and professional journeys.

To successfully implement mentorship and accountability into your life, begin by prayerfully identifying potential mentors and accountability partners. Seek individuals who have experience in the areas you wish to grow, who demonstrate a strong faith and commitment to Kingdom principles, and who possess characteristics you admire. Approach these individuals with humility and respect, expressing your desire to learn from their experience and to build a mutually beneficial relationship. Be prepared to invest the necessary time and effort into nurturing the relationship. Remember, building trust and rapport takes time; patience and perseverance are key. Don't be discouraged if the initial connection doesn't feel like a perfect fit, continue to prayerfully seek guidance as you build these critical relationships.

Beyond the interpersonal dynamics, it's crucial to establish practical structures for accountability. This could involve setting clear goals, establishing regular check-in times, and utilizing tools such as shared documents or apps to track progress. Transparency and honesty are paramount; be willing to share both your successes and your struggles with your mentor or accountability partner. This openness allows for constructive feedback and support.

Building a thriving Kingdom community requires active participation and a commitment to mutual support. Mentorship and accountability aren't just helpful; they are essential elements for accelerating spiritual and professional growth. Embrace the opportunity to both give and receive mentorship, and to establish strong accountability partnerships. These relationships will provide invaluable support, guidance, and encouragement, propelling you towards the fulfillment of your God-given purpose and the creation of a life and business that glorifies God. Remember, the Kingdom is built not in isolation but in community, in the collaborative spirit of mutual support and shared growth. Embrace this community, nurture these relationships, and watch as your journey towards Kingdom acceleration is exponentially amplified. Let us pray for the grace and strength to build these vital relationships and to support each other on the path to Kingdom success.

Networking and Building Strategic Partnerships

Building upon the foundation of mentorship and accountability, we now delve into the crucial aspect of networking and forming strategic partnerships. These aren't merely social gatherings; they are strategic initiatives designed to expand your influence, access new opportunities, and build a powerful, collaborative Kingdom community focused on mutual success and spiritual growth. Think of it as extending the scaffolding of mentorship and accountability to create a broader, more robust structure capable of supporting even more ambitious goals and weathering even greater challenges.

Imagine a bustling networking event, filled with Christian entrepreneurs, leaders, and professionals, each brimming with unique skills, talents, and experiences. This isn't just about exchanging business cards; it's about connecting with individuals who share your faith and values, creating relationships based on mutual respect, trust, and a shared vision for Kingdom impact. It's about discovering synergistic partnerships – collaborations where the combined strengths of two or more individuals or organizations create a force far greater than the sum of its parts.

The key to effective networking within the Kingdom context lies in approaching it with a servant's heart. This isn't about what you can gain, but about what you can contribute. What unique gifts and talents has God given you? How can you use these to bless others and build up the Kingdom? When you approach networking with this mindset, you create a powerful magnetism that attracts opportunities and strengthens existing relationships.

Consider the parable of the talents in Matthew 25:14-30. The master entrusts his servants with varying amounts of talent, expecting them to use those talents wisely. Those who diligently used their talents were rewarded, while the one who buried his talent was condemned. This parable highlights the importance of actively using our gifts and talents to further God's Kingdom. Effective networking is an extension of this principle, a means of leveraging our unique abilities to impact others and amplify our reach.

Building strong, strategic partnerships involves more than just making connections; it requires careful cultivation and nurturing. It's about identifying individuals or organizations whose values align with yours, whose strengths complement your weaknesses, and whose goals are synergistic with your own. This alignment creates a solid foundation for a long-term, mutually beneficial relationship.

Consider the example of a Christian marketing agency partnering with a non-profit organization dedicated to providing clean water in developing countries. The agency could leverage its marketing expertise to create impactful campaigns, raising awareness and funds for the non-profit, while the non-profit could offer the agency a powerful platform to demonstrate its faith-based values and contribute to a tangible, world-changing cause. Both organizations benefit significantly from this synergistic collaboration.

The process of identifying potential partners requires thoughtful prayer and discernment. Begin by clearly defining your goals and objectives. What are you hoping to achieve through a partnership? What skills, resources, or expertise do you lack that a partner could provide? Once you have a clear understanding of your needs, you can begin to identify potential partners who could fill those gaps.

Attend industry events, conferences, and workshops specifically geared towards Christian entrepreneurs and professionals. These gatherings offer a fertile ground for networking and building connections with like-minded individuals. Actively listen to others, showing genuine interest in their work and their vision. Don't just focus on pitching your own business; instead, focus on how you can help others achieve their goals.

Online platforms and social media also provide valuable opportunities for connecting with potential partners. Engage in online communities and forums relevant to your industry and faith. Share your expertise, participate in discussions, and build relationships through meaningful interactions. This approach builds your credibility and expands your network without requiring extensive travel or large time commitments.

Once you've identified potential partners, initiate contact with them. Express your interest in collaborating and highlight the synergistic benefits of working together. Be prepared to offer a clear and concise proposal outlining the terms of the partnership, the goals to be achieved, and the responsibilities of each party. It is crucial to establish clear expectations and communication channels from the outset to prevent misunderstandings and conflicts.

Remember that building strong, lasting partnerships takes time and effort. It's a process of cultivating trust and developing a strong working relationship. Be patient, persistent, and proactive in maintaining communication and building rapport. Regular check-ins, shared goals, and collaborative projects will help strengthen the bond and ensure the partnership remains aligned with both parties' goals.

Beyond formal partnerships, informal collaborations can be equally beneficial. Offering support and assistance to other Christian entrepreneurs, sharing knowledge and resources, and offering constructive feedback are all powerful ways to build strong relationships within the community. This spirit of mutual support and encouragement is the hallmark of a thriving Kingdom community.

Remember, spiritual warfare is a reality, and this extends to the business world. Stay vigilant and prayerful, ensuring that all your partnerships are aligned with God's will and values. Pray for guidance in choosing partners, for wisdom in navigating potential challenges, and for the strength to persevere through difficulties. Seek God's discernment to avoid partnerships that could compromise your faith or values.

Building a thriving Kingdom community is a continuous process, not a destination. It requires ongoing effort, consistent prayer, and a commitment to serving others. As you cultivate your network and forge strategic partnerships, remember that the primary goal isn't just to achieve professional success but to use your talents and resources to glorify God and make a positive impact on the world. Embrace the journey, celebrate your successes, learn from your challenges, and continue to grow in faith and wisdom. Your Kingdom community will be a source of strength, support, and inspiration, propelling you towards a future of abundance and purpose, fulfilling the divine plan God has for your life and business. Let us pray for wisdom, guidance, and strength to build these relationships that will bless us and bless the Kingdom.

GIVING BACK AND SERVING OTHERS

The tapestry of a thriving Kingdom community isn't woven solely from strategic partnerships and networking; it's also richly embroidered with threads of service and giving back. While building strong professional relationships is crucial for growth and impact, the true measure of a kingdom-minded business lies in its commitment to uplifting others and contributing to the well-being of the broader community. This isn't merely an act of charity; it's a fundamental principle rooted in our faith, a reflection of God's boundless love and generosity.

Consider the profound impact of acts of service. When we give back, we're not simply providing assistance; we're participating in God's redemptive work in the world. We are mirroring His selfless love, extending His grace and compassion to those in need. This act of giving isn't just a moral imperative; it's a powerful catalyst for personal growth, spiritual enrichment, and even business prosperity.

Think of the parable of the Good Samaritan (Luke 10:25-37). The Samaritan, despite social and religious differences, demonstrated radical compassion and selfless service by tending to the injured man. This act, seemingly insignificant in its immediate context, embodies the very essence of kingdom living—a life dedicated to serving others without expectation of reward. This is the spirit we should emulate in our businesses and communities.

The benefits of giving back extend far beyond the recipients of our generosity. When we engage in philanthropic activities, we cultivate empathy, humility, and gratitude. We develop a deeper appreciation for the blessings in our own lives and a heightened awareness of the needs around us. This broadened perspective can significantly enrich our spiritual journey and deepen our relationship with God.

Consider how community engagement can strengthen your business. By actively participating in local initiatives, you build brand loyalty, foster positive relationships with your customers and stakeholders, and create a positive image within the community. This isn't just about generating goodwill; it's about cultivating genuine connections based on shared values and a common purpose. A community-minded business is viewed not simply as a profit-generating entity but as a valued member of the community, committed to its overall well-being.

But how do we practically integrate giving back into our busy schedules and already demanding businesses? The answer lies in intentionality and creative problem-solving. It doesn't require massive financial contributions or grandiose gestures; it begins with small, consistent acts of service, tailored to your unique skills and resources.

Perhaps you possess exceptional marketing skills. Offer your expertise pro bono to a local non-profit organization, designing and implementing effective marketing campaigns to enhance their reach and impact. If you have a talent for organizing, volunteer your time to coordinate a community event or fundraiser. Are you proficient in financial management? Offer your services to a local church or charity, providing guidance and support in managing their financial resources.

The possibilities are endless. The key is to identify your strengths and find ways to leverage them to serve others. This process often involves identifying local organizations aligned with your values and mission. Research local charities, community centers, and non-profits. Attend their events, connect with their leaders, and explore opportunities to contribute your talents and resources. Remember, prayer is crucial in discerning where God is leading you to serve.

Let's consider practical examples. A successful entrepreneur, blessed with financial abundance, might choose to establish a scholarship fund for underprivileged students, enabling them to pursue higher education. A team of software developers could create a pro bono mobile application for a local food bank, streamlining their operations and improving their outreach to the community. An experienced marketing professional might offer free marketing consultation to small, faith-based businesses, empowering them to grow and thrive. These are just a few examples; the possibilities are limited only by your imagination and willingness to serve.

Remember, the impact of giving isn't solely measured in monetary terms. Often, the most meaningful contributions are those that come from the heart—a listening ear, a helping hand, a word of encouragement. A simple act of kindness, a gesture of compassion, can make a profound difference in someone's life and strengthen the bonds within our Kingdom community.

Volunteering your time is an invaluable way to give back. Consider dedicating a set number of hours each week or month to a cause you're passionate about. This could involve working at a soup kitchen, visiting the elderly, mentoring at-risk youth, or participating in environmental cleanup initiatives. The experience is deeply rewarding, fostering personal growth and providing a sense of purpose beyond the confines of your business endeavors.

Furthermore, organizing a fundraising event for a worthy cause can bring together your network and community, fostering collaboration and a shared sense of purpose. Consider hosting a charity golf tournament, a bake sale, or a concert, leveraging your connections to maximize participation and donations. These events not only raise funds but also strengthen bonds within the community, creating a sense of unity and shared purpose.

But the act of giving back shouldn't be a sporadic, infrequent event. It should be integrated into the very fabric of your business, a core value that guides your decisions and shapes your interactions with the community. This requires a long-term commitment, a consistent dedication to serving others, and a willingness to embrace opportunities to make a difference. Incorporate acts of service into your business plan, allocating a portion of your profits to charitable causes or setting aside time for volunteer work. This demonstrates a commitment to social responsibility and strengthens your brand image.

Remember that the benefits of giving back are reciprocal. While you are serving others, you are simultaneously enriching your own life. The joy of giving, the fulfillment of making a difference, the strengthened community bonds, all contribute to a more meaningful and fulfilling existence. This is the essence of kingdom living—a life of service, generosity, and unwavering commitment to uplifting others, all while building a thriving and impactful business.

The journey of building a thriving Kingdom community is an ongoing process of growth, learning, and refinement. It's not a destination but a lifelong commitment to living out our faith in tangible ways. As we actively participate in serving others, we discover a deeper understanding of God's love and a stronger connection to our community. Through acts of service, we not only bless others but also experience the transformative power of giving, enriching our spiritual lives and strengthening our businesses. This symbiotic relationship between service and success is the heart of a truly thriving Kingdom community. Let's commit to prayerfully seeking opportunities to serve, generously sharing our resources, and consistently building a community that reflects the love and compassion of our Lord.

RESOURCES AND TOOLS FOR CONTINUED GROWTH

Additionally, building a thriving Kingdom community doesn't end with the closing of this chapter. It's a dynamic, ongoing process that requires continuous learning, growth, and support. To help you navigate this exciting path and continue building your Kingdom-focused business, I've compiled a wealth of resources and tools designed to empower and equip you for sustained success. Think of these as your allies in this journey – partners in prayer and progress.

First and foremost, consider the power of mentorship and coaching. Navigating the complexities of business and faith simultaneously can present unique challenges. A skilled Christian life coach can provide personalized guidance, support, and accountability, helping you to align your business strategies with your spiritual values. They can help you navigate difficult decisions, overcome obstacles, and stay focused on your God-given purpose. Many coaches specialize in faith-based entrepreneurship, offering tailored strategies for building kingdom businesses that are both profitable and purpose-driven. I strongly encourage you to seek out a coach who resonates with your values and who can provide the individualized support you need.

Investing in your personal and professional development is an essential part of this journey. A multitude of online courses and workshops cater specifically to Christian entrepreneurs and leaders. These programs offer practical instruction on topics such as financial management, marketing, leadership development, and spiritual warfare for business. Look for courses that integrate biblical principles with practical business strategies, helping you to build a faith-based business that aligns with your spiritual calling. Don't just passively consume information; actively apply what you're learning, testing and refining your strategies along the way.

Furthermore, consider the immense value of connecting with like-minded individuals. Joining a Christian business network or online community provides a supportive environment where you can share experiences, exchange ideas, and receive encouragement from fellow entrepreneurs who understand the unique challenges and rewards of building a faith-based enterprise. These communities offer a safe space to ask questions, seek advice, and celebrate successes. The collective wisdom and mutual support found in such networks are invaluable assets on your journey. These aren't just casual groups; they are strategic alliances built on shared faith and a common pursuit of excellence.

Networking opportunities within faith-based organizations are also incredibly beneficial. Attending conferences, seminars, and workshops organized by Christian business associations can provide invaluable networking opportunities, expose you to new ideas, and connect you with potential mentors and collaborators. Remember that these interactions are not just about transactional business; they're about building genuine relationships rooted in shared faith and a common purpose. Actively listen, offer your help, and nurture these relationships. You never know what doors God may open through a simple act of connection.

Beyond formal coaching and networking, remember the power of prayer and spiritual disciplines. Consistent prayer is not just a spiritual practice; it's a strategic tool for seeking guidance, wisdom, and protection in your business endeavors. Dedicate time each day for prayer and reflection, seeking God's direction in your decisions and aligning your actions with His will. Regular Bible study and meditation will further strengthen your spiritual foundation, providing the inner strength and resilience you need to overcome obstacles and persevere through challenges.

Consider developing a personal spiritual practice that goes beyond merely attending church services. This could involve daily devotional time, journaling your prayers and insights, or engaging in quiet reflection in nature. The goal is to cultivate a deep and abiding relationship with God, allowing His wisdom to guide your decisions and empower your actions. Such spiritual disciplines are not optional extras; they're foundational to building a truly thriving Kingdom community.

Access to relevant resources is crucial. Explore online platforms and libraries dedicated to Christian business and leadership resources.

Many websites offer articles, blog posts, podcasts, and books that address specific challenges and offer practical advice. Stay updated on the latest trends and best practices in your industry, while remaining rooted in your faith-based values. Learning shouldn't be a once-off event; it should be an ongoing commitment to personal and professional growth.

The importance of continuous learning cannot be overstated. Stay curious, be open to new ideas, and constantly seek opportunities to improve your skills and knowledge. Remember, your journey of building a thriving Kingdom community is a marathon, not a sprint. The ability to adapt, learn, and grow is critical to your long-term success.

Another invaluable resource is the wisdom found within the Bible itself. Regularly studying scriptures related to business, leadership, and stewardship will provide you with timeless principles that guide your actions and shape your decisions. This isn't about finding quick formulas for success; it's about aligning your business with God's principles of justice, integrity, and love. Look for biblical examples of successful leaders and businesses, understanding the spiritual principles that underpinned their success.

Furthermore, remember the power of accountability. Find a trusted mentor, a close friend, or a fellow entrepreneur who can provide accountability and support as you navigate the challenges and celebrate the successes of your journey. Sharing your experiences, both triumphs and setbacks, can provide invaluable perspective and encouragement. It's important to surround yourself with individuals who uplift you and challenge you to grow. Choose wisely those you allow to influence your decisions and actions.

The tools mentioned above are not just passive resources; they are active instruments in your hands to build and sustain a thriving Kingdom community. Use them strategically, consistently, and prayerfully. Remember, building a successful kingdom-focused business is not just about financial gain; it's about making a positive impact on the world while living out your faith.

Consider creating a dedicated space for continued learning and personal reflection. This could be a physical space in your home or office, or a digital space such as a dedicated folder on your computer or a special notebook. In this space, you can collect inspiring articles, journal your reflections, and store relevant resources. This will become your personal sanctuary of learning and growth, fostering a deeper connection with your faith and your entrepreneurial journey.

In conclusion, the journey towards building a thriving Kingdom community is a lifelong commitment to growth, service, and continuous learning. By utilizing the resources and tools provided, coupled with consistent prayer and spiritual disciplines, you can create a business that not only prospers financially but also reflects God's love and compassion in the world. Remember, you are not alone on this journey. Seek out the support of mentors, coaches, and fellow entrepreneurs, and embrace the power of community to achieve your God-given purpose. May God richly bless your efforts as you build His kingdom, one step at a time. This is not just a business venture; it's a sacred calling. Embrace it fully and watch God work through you in amazing ways.

FINAL PRAYERS AND DECLARATIONS FOR BUSINESS SUCCESS

Father God, as I stand at the precipice of continued growth and success in my business, I humbly come before You, acknowledging Your unwavering hand in all that I have accomplished thus far. I thank You for the wisdom, guidance, and strength You have bestowed upon me, enabling me to overcome obstacles and navigate the complexities of the business world while remaining steadfast in my faith. I give You praise for the opportunities that have come my way, for the partnerships that have strengthened my endeavors, and for the clients and customers who have supported my work.

I recognize that all my achievements are a testament to Your grace and provision. I surrender my business entirely to Your sovereign will, trusting in Your divine plan for its future. I pray for continued protection from any harm, deceit, or negativity that might seek to hinder my progress. Shield my business from financial setbacks, unforeseen challenges, and the destructive forces of competition that operate outside of Your ethical framework. I ask for Your guidance in every decision I make, ensuring that my actions always align with Your righteous principles and reflect the values of integrity, honesty, and compassion that are central to my Kingdom-focused business.

Grant me the wisdom to discern opportunities for growth and expansion while remaining vigilant against temptations that compromise my faith or my values. May I always seek Your counsel before embarking on new ventures, ensuring that they are in harmony with Your overarching plan for my life and my business. Bless my employees, collaborators, and partners with Your wisdom, strength, and guidance. May they always strive to work together in unity, harmony, and with an unwavering commitment to excellence.

I declare that my business will continue to prosper and flourish under Your divine blessing. I declare that it will be a beacon of light in the marketplace, a testament to Your power and a source of inspiration for others. I declare that my business will be a tool for Your kingdom, contributing to positive social change and impacting lives for Your glory. I declare an abundance of resources, both financial and spiritual, to sustain and expand my operations. I declare protection for my physical and mental well-being, ensuring that I am empowered to handle the challenges and responsibilities of business ownership with strength, grace, and resilience.

Father, I ask for Your continued blessings upon my family, providing them with the love, security, and emotional support they need amidst my busy schedule. Help me maintain a healthy work-life balance, prioritizing time with loved ones while remaining focused on my business objectives. I also pray for wisdom in managing my time effectively and efficiently, eliminating distractions and making optimal use of my resources.

I commit to maintaining a strong spiritual discipline, dedicating time each day for prayer, Bible study, and meditation. I will regularly seek guidance through prayer and engage in spiritual practices that enhance my relationship with You and provide strength in times of adversity. I know that my success is not solely based on my own efforts, but is reliant on Your favor, guidance, and provision.

I ask for the activation of my spiritual gifts in the context of my business. Grant me discernment, wisdom, strategic thinking, and the ability to communicate effectively with my team and clients. Grant me patience, empathy, and the ability to navigate complex interpersonal dynamics with grace and understanding. Help me to model a Christ-like leadership style, fostering collaboration, mutual respect, and an environment of positivity and productivity.

I renounce any negative patterns of thinking or behaving that have hindered my success in the past. I release all fears, doubts, and anxieties that seek to limit my potential. I declare my mind renewed and transformed by the power of Your Holy Spirit. I am confident in Your plan for my life and my business, and I embrace the challenges ahead with courage, faith, and a steadfast reliance on Your guidance.

May my business be a testament to Your goodness and a reflection of Your love. May it bring honor and glory to Your name, and may I always be a faithful steward of the resources You have entrusted to me. I pray for the protection of my business from all forms of injustice, corruption, or unethical practices. May my business dealings always be transparent, honest, and in alignment with Your highest standards of ethical conduct.

I declare that my business will operate with integrity, honesty, and transparency. I will treat all my employees, clients, and partners with fairness, respect, and compassion. I will strive to create a work environment that is safe, inclusive, and supportive, fostering a sense of community and belonging. I commit to conducting my business in a way that demonstrates Your love and compassion to the world.

I pray for the wisdom to make sound financial decisions, managing my resources effectively and avoiding wasteful spending. I commit to using my financial resources wisely, not only for the growth of my business but also for supporting charitable causes that align with my faith and values. I declare that my business will be financially sound and profitable, enabling me to provide for my family and contribute to the Kingdom's work.

Furthermore, I declare that my business will be a place of spiritual growth and development for myself and my employees. I will create an environment where faith is welcomed, encouraged, and integrated into our daily work. I will provide opportunities for spiritual enrichment through team prayer, devotional meetings, and acts of service. I pray for the spiritual maturity and growth of my team, enabling them to thrive personally and professionally. I pray for ongoing guidance in creating a business environment that promotes spiritual growth and encourages the integration of faith into every aspect of work.

I pray for the protection of my family and my business from any unforeseen accidents, illnesses, or calamities. I ask for Your divine intervention in times of crisis, providing comfort, strength, and guidance in navigating difficult circumstances. I declare that Your peace will transcend all anxieties and fears, and I place my trust in Your sovereign plan for my future.

Father, I pray that my business will serve as a powerful tool for spreading the Gospel and making a difference in the world. I pray that I may be granted opportunities to share my faith with those I encounter in my business, always exhibiting a spirit of love, respect, and understanding. I declare that my business will be a force for good in the world, impacting lives for Your glory.

As I conclude this time of prayer, I thank You for Your immeasurable love, grace, and provision. I commit to walking in Your ways, trusting in Your promises, and following Your guidance. I am confident that with Your help, I can build a thriving Kingdom community that brings honor and glory to Your name. Amen.

THE FINAL RELEASE

Acknowledgements

First and foremost, I offer my heartfelt gratitude to God Almighty, the source of all wisdom, strength, and inspiration. This book would not exist without His divine guidance and unwavering support. My family, particularly my daughter Jasmyn, Grandson Augustine, Granddaughter Ariah, parents, relatives who have been my constant source of encouragement and love throughout this journey. Their patience, understanding, and unwavering belief in me have been invaluable.

I am deeply appreciative to my editor Cha, whose expertise and insights have significantly enriched this work. Your key to detail, patience, cooperation and encouragement kept me motivated to complete the book, regardless of the obstacles that I had faced. Thank you for your invaluable contributions. Finally, a special thank you to all those who have supported my ministry and business over the years; your prayers and encouragement have been a constant source of strength.

APPENDIX

This appendix contains supplementary materials to enhance your *Kingdom Acceleration* journey. Each section is designed to deepen your spiritual walk, strengthen your mindset, and equip you with divine tools to thrive as a Kingdom entrepreneur.

Appendix A: Expanded Prayer List

A collection of powerful prayers designed to help you overcome life's challenges and align your heart with God's divine plan. These prayers cover business decisions, leadership challenges, financial needs, relationship healing, and spiritual breakthroughs. Each one is written to remind you that God is your ultimate source of wisdom, provision, and peace.

Appendix B: 10 Powerful Kingdom Entrepreneur Prayers

Ten intentional prayers written to equip Kingdom entrepreneurs with faith, strategy, and supernatural guidance. These prayers focus on divine creativity, integrity, purpose, and prosperity—helping you remain grounded in your mission while expanding your influence for God's glory.

Appendix C: 20 Affirmations and Declarations

A life-giving collection of affirmations and declarations to renew your mind and activate your faith. Each statement empowers you to speak success, favor, and breakthrough over your business, mindset, and spiritual walk—anchoring your identity in God's promises and abundance.

Expanded Prayer List

This section contains a powerful collection of prayers to guide you through the different seasons and challenges of your Kingdom Acceleration journey.

Each prayer invites you to connect deeply with the Holy Spirit and call forth divine wisdom, strength, and peace.

Prayer for Divine Direction

Heavenly Father, lead me in Your will and not my own. Order my steps and make my path clear. Help me to discern Your voice above all others and follow where You lead with faith and confidence. Amen.

Prayer for Business Clarity and Growth

Lord, bless the work of my hands and let every idea You have given me produce fruit in due season. Remove confusion and fear, and replace them with strategy, structure, and supernatural favor. Amen.

Prayer for Financial Breakthrough

Father, I declare overflow and provision over every area of my life. Close every door of lack and open the windows of Heaven. Teach me to be a wise steward and a cheerful giver. Amen.

Prayer for Relationships and Alignment

God, surround me with those who uplift, encourage, and align with Your purpose for my life. Remove distractions and unhealthy attachments that hinder my growth. Amen.

Prayer for Healing and Restoration

Lord, heal the broken areas within me—my heart, mind, body, and soul. Restore what was lost or stolen, and give me the strength to move forward with joy and peace. Amen.

Prayer for Overcoming Adversity

Father, even when I cannot see the outcome, I trust that You are fighting for me. Use every trial to build endurance, patience, and faith. Amen.

Prayer for Kingdom Expansion

God, use my life, my voice, and my business as instruments for Your Kingdom. May my influence draw others closer to You and create generational impact. Amen.

Prayer for Wisdom and Discernment

Holy Spirit, grant me the wisdom to make sound decisions and the discernment to recognize opportunities sent by You. Let me never lean on my own understanding. Amen.

Prayer for Peace and Balance

Lord, when life feels overwhelming, remind me that You are my peace. Help me rest in Your presence and prioritize what matters most. Amen.

Prayer for Acceleration and Favor

Father, thank You for divine acceleration. Let doors open that no man can shut. Release supernatural favor over my life, business, and purpose. Amen.

APPENDIX B

10 Powerful Kingdom Entrepreneur Prayers

Prayer for Vision –

Lord, renew my vision daily. Keep me focused on what You've called me to build and not distracted by worldly success.

Prayer for Integrity –

Help me to operate my business with honesty, excellence, and honor so that others see You through my actions.

Prayer for Creativity –

Breathe divine inspiration into every project and idea, making them unique reflections of Your glory.

Prayer for Divine Partnerships –

Align me with clients, investors, and partners who carry the same Kingdom values and purpose.

Prayer for Endurance –

Strengthen me when progress seems slow. Help me to remain steadfast, knowing Your timing is perfect.

Prayer for Abundance –

Release overflow so that I can give, sow, and serve without limitation.

Prayer for Boldness –

Give me courage to step into new territories and release what You've placed inside me with confidence.

Prayer for Wisdom in Stewardship –

Teach me to manage resources with grace and accountability, ensuring every decision honors You.

Prayer for Expansion –

Enlarge my territory, Lord. Let my business reach nations and impact souls for Your Kingdom.

Prayer for Legacy –

May what I build today bless generations to come and carry Your name into the future. Amen.

APPENDIX C

20 Affirmations and Declarations

1. I am divinely chosen and equipped to prosper in my purpose.
2. God's favor surrounds my life and business like a shield.
3. I walk in divine wisdom, clarity, and strategy every day.
4. I attract divine connections that align with my Kingdom assignment.
5. My faith produces fruit and supernatural results.
6. I am a vessel of excellence, creativity, and Kingdom influence.
7. Lack and limitation have no authority in my life.
8. I am a faithful steward of every resource God entrusts to me.
9. I speak life, abundance, and victory into every area of my business.
10. God's timing accelerates my progress without striving.
11. I operate from peace, not pressure.
12. My words carry the power of breakthrough and creation.
13. I am anointed to lead with love, wisdom, and compassion.
14. Every challenge is an opportunity for greater growth and glory.
15. I am connected to divine wealth and supernatural provision.

16. I radiate joy, excellence, and God's presence in all I do.
17. The Holy Spirit is my ultimate business partner.
18. I am walking in divine acceleration and Kingdom favor.
19. My legacy will reflect God's goodness and grace.
20. I declare that my life and business will glorify God and impact nations.

FINAL ENCOURAGEMENT AND CLOSING PRAYER

As you complete Kingdom Acceleration, remember that this is not the end of your journey—it is the divine beginning of your release, your increase, and your next level of purpose. Everything you have endured was preparation. Every delay was divine. Every lesson was positioning you to lead, prosper, and impact lives through your obedience.

You are no longer standing in waiting—you are walking in acceleration.

God has already set your miracle in motion. Continue to trust Him when you cannot trace Him, and continue to build even when you cannot see the full picture. Your faith is your key to forward motion.

You are the evidence of God's promise fulfilled. You are the seed of generational change. You are the Kingdom leader He chose for such a time as this.

Closing Prayer

Heavenly Father,

Thank You for every reader who has walked through this journey of faith, purpose, and acceleration. May their hearts remain steadfast in Your will. Open doors that no man can shut. Release supernatural wisdom, divine strategy, and unstoppable favor upon their lives and businesses.

Let this book become a living testimony of transformation—spiritually, mentally, and financially.

Bless them to be the chain-breakers, the restorers, and the generational trailblazers You've called them to be.

In Jesus' mighty name, Amen.

Stay Connected

For more encouragement, coaching, and Kingdom resources:

HealingWithinTransformationCenter.com – The main hub for faith-based growth, healing and empowerment for personal transformation.

AlishaJacksonAcademy.com – Join certification courses, eCourses, and life coaching programs.

FaithConnectionCenter.org – Connect with domestic violence survivors and their children under 5 years old outreach programs and community events.

Follow Ms. Alisha Jackson, MSW on social media:

TikTok | YouTube → @DrAlishaJackson

Kingdom Acceleration Glossary

"But seek first the Kingdom of God and His righteousness, and all these things shall be added to you."

-Matthew 6:33 (NKJV)

Kingdom-Focused Business

A business operated according to biblical principles, prioritizing faith, integrity, and service to others.

Spiritual Warfare

The divine battle between good and evil where believers use prayers, fasting, and faith as weapons of victory through Christ.

Spiritual Gifts

God-given abilities empowered by the Holy Spirit to serve, build, and advance His Kingdom purpose.

Kingdom Confidence

A deep trust in God's promises that produces boldness, courage, and peace even in the face of adversity.

Renewing the Mind

The process of transforming your thoughts to align with God's Word and Kingdom truth.

Emotional Intelligence

The spiritual maturity to discern, manage, and express emotions in ways that reflect Christ's character.

CBT (Christian Based Thinking)

Replacing negative thoughts with God's truth through scriptural reflection and faith-based mindset renewal.

Forgiveness

Choosing to release others and yourself through the grace of Christ, freeing your heart to receive healing and peace.

Gratitude

A daily attitude of thankfulness that unlocks joy, contentment, and divine favor.

Bondage

Any spiritual or emotional chain that keeps you from walking in the full freedom Christ has already given.

Adversity

The refining process God uses to strengthen faith, build endurance, and reveal divine purpose.

Faith

Complete trust in God's will and timing, believing that His promises are already working in your favor.

Conqueror

One who overcomes every obstacle through Christ's power, walking boldly in Kingdom authority.

Testimony

A personal story of God's deliverance and faithfulness that brings glory to Him and encouragement to others.

Self-Reflection

The spiritual practice of examining your heart, thoughts, and actions in light of God's truth for continual growth.

Entrepreneurial Journey

Building and stewarding God-inspired visions with integrity, purpose, and faith-driven strategy.

Spiritual Weapons

The divine tools-prayers, fasting, Scripture, worship, and faith-used to stand firm against spiritual attacks.

Financial Stewardship

Managing God's resources with wisdom, obedience, and generosity to advance His Kingdom.

References

All Scripture quotations in this book are drawn from the Holy Bible. Unless otherwise noted, verses are quoted from the King James Version (KJV).

Matthew 6:33 is referenced from the New King James Version (NKJV).

The Word of God serves as the foundation of Kingdom Acceleration, providing divine wisdom, instruction, and revelation for those pursuing spiritual growth and Kingdom purpose.

The Holy Bible, New King James Version. (1982). Thomas Nelson.

(Matthew 6:33)

The Holy Bible, King James Version. (1769/2017). Cambridge University Press.

(Matthew 25:14–30; Luke 10:25–37; Psalm 139:14; Philippians 4:13; Ephesians 2:10; Ephesians 6:10–18; Psalm 147:3; Romans 8:28; Matthew 5:23–24; Ephesians 4:2–3; Colossians 3:12–15; Proverbs 16:3; Philippians 4:6–7; Psalm 23; Proverbs 3:5–6; Philippians 4:19)

Author Biography

Ms. Alisha Jackson, MSW is a charismatic Christian Life Coach, motivational speaker, author, and visionary entrepreneur called to break generational curses and guide others into Kingdom abundance. Born from humble beginnings, Alisha's journey was one of resilience, faith, and divine transformation. She overcame cycles of poverty, rejection, and adversity through an unwavering trust in God's promises and an unshakable belief in her divine purpose.

With over 20 years of professional human services and ministry experience, Alisha has dedicated her life to helping others heal from emotional wounds, rebuild their faith, and rediscover their God-given identity. As the founder of **Healing Within Transformation Center**, she has created a global faith-based hub that empowers individuals to rise above limitation and walk boldly in their Kingdom calling.

Through her coaching programs, books, and speaking engagements, Ms. Jackson teaches powerful biblical principles on faith, mindset renewal, inner healing, and financial stewardship. Her mission is not only to inspire others to dream again but to equip them with the practical tools and spiritual strategies to manifest those dreams through Kingdom alignment.

She stands as a living testimony that no matter your past, your pain can be turned into purpose—and your obedience can birth legacy. Alisha's compassionate spirit and prophetic insight continue to transform lives, restore families, and ignite movements that advance the Kingdom of God.

Connect with Ms. Alisha Jackson, MSW at:

Website: **HealingWithinTransformationCenter.com**

Website: **AlishaJacksonAcademy.com**

Website: **FaithConnectionCenter.org**

Social Media: YouTube | TikTok **@DrAlishaJackson**